STORYTELLING FOR
LEADERSHIP & INFLUENCE

"As a filmmaker and media consultant, I've seen firsthand how much communication has changed in our lifetime. Yet many professional communicators never adjusted. *Storytelling for Leadership & Influence* offers a clear roadmap for sharing your message in today's digital, distracted culture — and for doing so with relevance, purpose, and impact."

Phil Cooke, Ph.D.

Filmmaker, media consultant, and author of *Ideas on a Deadline: How to be Creative When the Clock is Ticking*

STORYTELLING FOR LEADERSHIP & INFLUENCE

HOW LEADERS FRAME MEANING, SHAPE THE MOMENT, AND REBUILD WHEN THE STORY BREAKS

Jeff Evans

STORYTELLING FOR LEADERSHIP & INFLUENCE
How Leaders Frame Meaning, Shape the Moment, and Rebuild When the Story Breaks

Published by Twin Tails Press, an imprint of JC Evans Inc.

Hardcover (Case Laminate): ISBN 979-8-9944297-0-9
Hardcover (Dust Jacket):   ISBN 979-8-9944297-3-0
Paperback: ISBN 979-8-9944297-1-6
eBook: ISBN 979-8-9944297-2-3

Printed in the United States of America.

Cover design and interior layout by JC Evans Inc.

Scripture quotations taken from the Holy Bible, New International Version®, NIV®. Copyright ©1973, 1978, 1984, 2011 by Biblica, Inc.™ Used by permission. All rights reserved worldwide.

This is a work of nonfiction. Some names and identifying details may have been changed to protect privacy.

A foreword may be included in future editions.

First Edition: 2026

To my wife, Cathy —
my companion in every season,
my reminder that time is borrowed,
and the reason I returned to the calling I had nearly forgotten.

"*The purposes of a person's heart are deep waters,*
but one who has insight draws them out."
Proverbs 20:5 (NIV)

"*The world changes according to the way people see it, and if*
you can alter, even by a millimeter, the way people look at reality,
then you can change the world."
James Baldwin

Contents

Introduction — Every Leader Is a Storyteller

PART I — CLARITY: THE MOTORCADE LESSON

Chapter 1 — The Rally on the Diag 3

Chapter 2 — Reagan, Kemp, and the Call 11

Chapter 3 — The Motorcade 15

    Leadership Reflection: Clarity Holds the Formation 23

    How to Apply This: Name the Moment 25

PART II — PRECISION: THE MARINE ONE LESSON

Chapter 4 — The Silent Language of Precision 31

Chapter 5 — Precision Is Communication 35

Chapter 6 — Forklifts and Shopping Malls 39

    Leadership Reflection: Silent Authority and Earned Trust 45

    How to Apply This: Make Precision Visible 47

PART III — NARRATIVE: HOW FRAMING DECIDES THE OUTCOME

Chapter 7 — The Last Rancher 53

Chapter 8 — Blank Spaces 61

Chapter 9 — The Movement That Split Itself 69

    Leadership Reflection: The Fight Over Meaning 83

    How to Apply This: Own the Frame 85

Part IV — The Human Story: Failure, Faith & Reinvention

Chapter 10 — The Film That Almost Happened 91

Chapter 11 — When the Floor Gives Way............................. 97

Chapter 12 — The Story You Tell Yourself.......................... 101

Leadership Reflection: The Story Beneath the Story 113

How to Apply This: Living One Story 115

Part V — Positioning & Purpose: The Formation of Influence

Chapter 13 — The Recall: The Win You Don't Receive 121

Chapter 14 — Influence From Outside the Frame 131

Chapter 15 — CfaN: Purpose as Strategic Positioning 139

Chapter 16 — When Purpose Meets Crisis........................... 143

Leadership Reflection: The Invisible Gravity of Influence........... 151

How to Apply This: Choose the Ground 155

Part VI — Restoration, Wonder & Future Story

Chapter 17 — The Road Back to Wonder 161

Chapter 18 — Story as Legacy..................................... 169

Chapter 19 — The Architecture of Accountability................... 173

Leadership Reflection: Wonder Recovered 179

How to Apply This: Restoration That Endures 183

Epilogue — Return to the Motorcade.............................. 187

EVERY LEADER IS A STORYTELLER

I didn't grow up dreaming about politics or leadership. The earliest clues about where my life would eventually bend were found in a place far removed from campaigns, conventions, or motorcades. They lived in the glow of studio lights and the thin electric tension that settles over a television set seconds before the cameras come alive.

In junior high and high school, I loved being on stage. I loved the transformation that happened when an audience leaned forward and the world became whatever the story demanded. Acting wasn't a detour for me. It was formation. It taught me how story lives inside people, how words create meaning, and how presence can steady a moment or break it apart.

My mom played a part in this long before I knew it would matter. She made a leap into television when I was young, and that leap reshaped our family's world. One day she was the stay-at-home mom; the next she was co-hosting a daytime talk show called *Day by Day*. She learned to navigate live call-ins, laugh with guests, improvise when a segment fell apart, and carry herself with a confidence she never had time to question. Watching her move from the kitchen table to the television studio taught me that transformation isn't always loud. Sometimes it's as simple as someone deciding the story of their life can grow larger.

Television sets have a pulse — a hum of cables, whispered instructions, shifting lights, and hurried improvisations that all somehow merge into something the audience experiences as smooth and intentional. Behind the scenes, though, every moment feels like it hangs by a thread.

When I was thirteen, I stepped into that tension for the first time. My mother was hosting one of her live call-in shows, and the crew invited me to floor direct the show. The production coordinator handed me a headset and pointed to my place on the edge of the set. He gave me a quick run-through of hand signals. The studio around me buzzed with frantic preparation — technicians checking cameras, staff rushing to last-minute details, phones ringing with early callers. I felt the excitement of it, but also the weight. This wasn't a rehearsal. There were no do-overs.

The director drifted in moments before the opening, confident in a way I later learned was less about talent and more about habit. He barked a few instructions, glanced at the monitors, and signaled to roll the music. The lights warmed. My mother straightened. I heard the word through my headset. I lifted my hand to cue her in, and she began speaking with the calm confidence of someone who had found her place in the world.

And then everything changed.

A sudden burst of profanity exploded through my headset — sharp, frantic, unmistakably angry. I felt my stomach drop. I was only thirteen, and to me that stream of fury sounded like accusation. I was sure I had done something wrong. But the show continued, and so did I — following every cue, steadying myself as the moment demanded.

When the broadcast ended and the headsets were lifted away, I finally learned the truth. The director, in his haste, had put the wrong title graphic on the air. It had nothing to do with me. What I experienced as personal failure was simply the chaos created by a leader who hadn't prepared.

That night etched something into me long before I had language for it: when a leader fails to bring clarity, confusion fills the space; and when confusion comes, someone must steady the moment.

I didn't yet know that lesson would follow me for the rest of my life.

Years later, as I walked onto the campus of the University of Michigan, I still thought my future might unfold behind a news desk. Storytelling felt like the most meaningful kind of work — helping people understand a confusing world through narrative clarity. But then another voice entered my life. Ronald Reagan captured my imagination not because of politics, but because of the way he spoke. His words lifted people. They carried warmth, optimism, and an ability to interpret the American story in a way that made sense of the moment.

Storytelling was no longer something that happened only on a stage or a television set. I saw it happening in rallies, in strategy rooms, in conversations between volunteers. Then there was the quiet confidence of Congressman Jack Kemp explaining economic policy with a grin that made ordinary people feel part of something larger. Politics introduced me to a different kind of storytelling — one with real stakes and consequences.

My path took turns I could never have predicted: campaigns and caucuses;

global crusades with Evangelist Reinhard Bonnke; moments of crisis in Ethiopia and India; late-night war rooms; quiet seasons of collapse; long stretches of reinvention; and ultimately the seven-year journey across the country that restored my sense of wonder. At every turning point, the same pattern revealed itself again and again: people follow the story that helps them make sense of the moment.

Sometimes that story is clear and empowering. Sometimes it's fractured and confusing. Sometimes it lifts people; sometimes it divides them. But it always shapes them.

Leadership, I eventually realized, is not fundamentally about authority or technique. It is about the interpretation of experience. It's about the way a leader helps people understand the world around them — what matters, what doesn't, where they are, and where they're going.

This book is not a memoir, even though it draws from my life. It's not a textbook, though it contains principles. It is a guided journey through moments that taught me what leadership really requires: the ability to tell the right story at the right time, with clarity, integrity, and presence.

Some of the stories ahead are exhilarating. Some are painful. Some unfolded on global stages; others took place in quiet rooms or unexpected corners of America. But all of them revealed something essential about human behavior, influence, and meaning.

This book is organized in six parts. Parts I-III explore external leadership — how you create clarity, precision, and narrative coherence for others. Part IV shifts inward to examine what happens when a leader's internal and external stories fall out of alignment. Parts V-VI explore how leaders rebuild influence through strategic positioning and the patient work of restoration.

Each part follows the same structure: story, reflection, application. The stories are drawn from my life — from presidential campaigns to ministry work to personal crisis. The reflections connect experience to principle. The applications provide frameworks you can use in your own leadership.

The structure is deliberate. Before you can lead others with authentic influence, you must first align who you are with what you project. Most leadership books teach external techniques. This one asks you to do harder work: to examine the story underneath the story.

My hope is simple: that as you walk through these scenes with me, you will begin to see leadership not as a title or a position, but as a narrative craft — one that shapes the people around you every day, whether you realize it or not.

Every leader is a storyteller. And every story — yours included — has the power to move people to action.

Let's begin.

PART I

CLARITY:
THE MOTORCADE LESSON

CHAPTER 1

THE RALLY ON THE DIAG: STEPPING INTO THE GAP

The University of Michigan is a place where history never quite settles into the past.

You feel it in the architecture — those tall, watchful buildings of brick and stone that had seen generations rise and fall. You feel it in the way students move through the campus, as if walking across a stage built long before they were born. And you feel it most powerfully on the Diag.

The Diag is the crossroads of everything — an open lawn cut by intersecting paths that funnels thousands of students through its heart every day. It's impossible to cross it without catching fragments of conversation, protest chants, guitar strums, political arguments, or philosophical debates. On that stretch of grass, the free speech movement had etched its early marks. Tom Hayden had once stood where students toss frisbees now, rallying the emerging wave of the New Left. The Students for a Democratic Society had taken shape here, shaping discussions that spilled far beyond Ann Arbor. It's a landscape haunted by megaphones and conviction.

By the time I arrived in the early 1980s, the upheavals of the sixties were already being turned into lecture anecdotes and nostalgic asides, but they hadn't really faded. They had simply hardened into assumptions. The default setting on campus was left-of-center. If you were conservative, you learned quickly that you were in the minority and that most people found that vaguely amusing.

Some professors wore their ideology on their sleeves. Others wrapped it in careful language and footnotes. You could sit through an entire economics lecture and feel the subtle pressure pushing you toward a single conclusion. In other classes, the ideology was overt. The heroes and villains were clearly cast. Ronald Reagan occupied a special place in that pantheon, and it was rarely favorable.

Still, even in that climate, there were bright points of intellectual honesty

— professors who insisted on real argument rather than ritual agreement, who welcomed dissent if you could back it up. Those classrooms gave me a strange sort of courage. I didn't always win the arguments, but I learned that truth doesn't collapse just because it's outnumbered.

Outside the lecture halls, life went on: football Saturdays, late nights at the library, cheap pizza, anxiety about exams. The campus could feel almost apolitical for long stretches. Then something would hit the bloodstream and remind everyone that Michigan had a tradition to maintain. Protests would spring up on the Diag. Card tables would multiply. Megaphones would emerge from nowhere.

In the fall of 1984, Walter Mondale's presidential campaign became one of those catalysts.

Gary Hart had electrified Ann Arbor earlier in the year when he launched his Michigan campaign before a vibrant crowd at the Michigan Union. In a town like this, Hart was more than a candidate; he was a cultural event. When he lost the nomination to Mondale, it felt to many students as if the adults had once again seized the wheel from the idealists.

The Mondale campaign needed a way to mend that rupture. They chose the most symbolic stage they could find: the Diag.

A unity rally was announced for late October. Gary Hart would return to campus, not as Mondale's rival but as his ally, standing in front of the same students who had once chanted his name and asking them to throw their energy behind the ticket that had beaten him. The Mondale team wanted a visual: a sea of students, a campus that had been Hart's stronghold now cheering for Mondale, cameras capturing the moment and broadcasting party unity across the state.

The rally wasn't just about Mondale; it was about reclaiming the story. If they could stage a massive show of support on a campus that had loved Hart, they could demonstrate that the party was united, that the young idealists had fallen in line.

The story they wanted was clear:

Mondale had the campus.

Mondale had the momentum.

Mondale had the future.

My roommate, Mike Davidson, and I saw something else: a blank space in the frame.

Ann Arbor might be a liberal town, but it wasn't monolithic. There were conservatives in the dorms, in the classrooms, and quietly sitting through lectures that mocked the man they admired. Reagan had his supporters here, and I was one of them.

As soon as we heard about the unity rally, Mike and I started talking about a counter-presence. A visible reminder, on camera, that this campus wasn't entirely in the tank for Mondale. We wanted Reagan signs in the shot. We wanted the television audience to see that the story of Michigan students in 1984 was more complicated than a single rally could suggest.

The obvious place to start was the College Republicans.

Their office was tucked away in the Michigan League, one of the older, historic buildings on the north side of central campus. On a good day, it might hold a couple of students and a stack of flyers. On the day we first knocked, it held nothing at all.

We knocked and waited. No answer.

We went back a few hours later. Still nothing.

The second time, we dug a pen out of a backpack, found a piece of scrap paper, and scrawled a note.

"Big Mondale rally next week. We need a counter-rally. Call us."

We slid it under the door and left.

The next day, nothing had changed. The hallway was still quiet. The door was still closed. We knocked again. Silence. We left another note, more urgent this time, again with our phone number.

On the third day, the door was open. One lone student manned a desk. The room was exactly what you'd expect: a handful of mismatched chairs, a couple of disorganized desks, and a few campaign posters. It didn't look like the nerve center of anything. It looked like a club that used to be active and now existed mostly as an entry on a list of student organizations.

We made our pitch. He was excited. We were excited. "Let's do this!"

By that evening, a small cluster of College Republicans had been pulled into the idea. We gathered materials and made signs. There's something strangely satisfying about the physicality of political preparation. The smell of markers and paint, the sound of tape tearing from the roll. It feels like building tools for an argument you haven't made yet.

Mike and I determined we would get to the Diag early and claim the best ground. Our goal was to be directly in the line of sight of the television cameras.

The morning of the rally, the campus felt oddly still when we stepped out of our apartment. It was one of those fall days when the air is gentle, and the light seems to soften the edges of everything. We carried our signs under our arms and walked toward the Diag with the kind of nervous energy you get before an exam you actually studied for.

We arrived long before the crowd did. The stage was already set up, a rectangular platform with a podium and risers for dignitaries. Crew members tested microphones, ran cables, and adjusted banners. A few people in Mondale gear moved about with clipboards and a certain proprietary air. They glanced at us, at our Reagan shirts and signs, and then looked away, as if we were a minor annoyance that could be dealt with later.

We went straight to the spot we had mapped out in our heads: just off-axis from the podium, where cameras could easily capture us. We planted our signs and waited.

Slowly, our side began to grow. A couple of friends joined us, then a few more. Then someone showed up with rolls of official Reagan-Bush stickers. We began distributing them in a frenzy. More and more students arrived, and many wanted Reagan stickers.

Then the first buses arrived.

They pulled up along the curb in a neat row, doors opening in sequence. Students in Mondale shirts and buttons poured out carrying pre-printed signs. They had the numbers. They had the sense of being on the side of the story everyone had already agreed upon.

For a moment, it felt as if we might be swallowed.

But as the minutes ticked by, the balance began to shift in a way that wasn't obvious to the rally organizers on the stage but was very obvious to us on the ground. More people drifted toward our side of the lawn. Some were openly conservative. Others were simply skeptical of the script. And then, as if summoned by some invisible signal, the pro-life crowd arrived.

They came with their own signs, their own chants, their own rhythm. They weren't part of the College Republicans. They weren't carrying Reagan posters. They were focused on a single issue, and they were loud. Whatever one thought of their approach, there was no denying their impact on the atmosphere.

Suddenly, the Diag didn't feel like a stage carefully dressed for a scripted unity rally. It felt contested. Instead of a single, clean narrative — Mondale and Hart, reconciled and moving forward together with a grateful student body — we now had a swirl of competing messages. Mondale. Reagan. Pro-life. Pro-choice. The tidy picture fractured into something far messier and, frankly, far more honest.

From the perspective of the television cameras, it must have looked cha-otic and vibrant at once. A candidate for president standing where Tom Hayden once rallied students, speaking into a microphone while a large portion of the crowd waved signs for the man he was running against. Protest banners bob-bing beside campaign posters. Chants colliding.

When Hart stepped up to speak, he attempted to be his charming, articu-late self. From our side of the lawn, we answered him with our own commen-tary, shouted across the crowd. It wasn't hateful or crude. It was college-aged bravado, sharpened by conviction and the thrill of being heard. We cheered for Reagan when his name came up. We mocked Mondale. We reminded anyone within earshot why we believed the country was better off staying the course.

When Mondale himself spoke, you could feel the weight of the race bear-ing down on him. The polls were not kind. Reagan's "Morning in America" narrative was sweeping the country, casting everything in a warm, optimis-tic glow. Mondale had facts and arguments. Reagan had a story that people wanted to inhabit. Even on that friendly campus, on that warm fall day, the tension between those two realities was palpable.

The real turning point, for me, came when I noticed the cameras.

Near the edge of the crowd, just beyond the first ranks of signs, the local news crews were working their way across the Diag. Their operators panned deliberately, searching for the images that would define the rally in a twen-ty-second clip. For most of the afternoon, their lenses had been trained on the podium — on Mondale and Hart, on the visuals the campaign had carefully arranged.

Then, one by one, the cameras swung toward us.

I remember lifting my sign a little higher — not out of vanity, but out of recognition. The notes slid under a locked door. The hours painting poster-board. The decision to arrive early and claim our ground. All of it had quietly crossed a threshold. What had begun as private conviction had become public reality.

When the speeches ended and the crowd began to dissolve, the adrenaline drained slowly. Mike and I walked back to our apartment hoarse, exhilarated, and unusually quiet. It had been fun, yes — but more than that, it had been revealing. We had watched a moment designed to tell one story fracture into something more complicated simply because we showed up with intention and timing.

The confirmation came the next morning.

The Ann Arbor News carried the rally across its front page. There were Mondale and Hart, framed exactly as the organizers had hoped. But woven into the image were our Reagan-Bush signs — visual proof that the campus narrative was not as settled as it had appeared.

The Detroit News ran its own photograph. Different angle. Same result. The unity rally had not emerged as a clean, unified image. It had emerged as a snapshot of a country in the middle of an argument.

The thrill wasn't seeing myself in print. It was seeing evidence that presence matters, that a small group, without budget, title, or permission, could alter the emotional center of a moment simply by standing in the right place at the right time.

Looking back, I can see that day as my true inciting incident — the moment leadership stopped being theoretical and became practical. No one appointed me. No one handed me authority. There was no credential, no role, no permission slip.

There was only a gap between the story being told and the reality I saw, and a choice to stand in it.

> There was only a gap between the story
> being told and the reality I saw,
> and a choice to stand in it.

That is the quiet truth at the heart of leadership: it often begins long before authority arrives. It begins when someone notices the frame is incomplete and decides not to let it pass unchallenged.

The Diag rally taught me that influence doesn't wait for credentials. It waits for courage — the courage to knock on doors that may not open, to leave notes that might be ignored, to gather a handful of people when the other side is bussing in hundreds, to arrive early, choose your ground, and hold steady when the cameras finally turn.

That warm fall day in 1984 wasn't only about Mondale or Hart or Reagan. It was about discovering that stepping into the gap changes the gravitational pull of a moment.

I walked onto the Diag that morning as a volunteer.

I walked away with the first hint that I might one day be a leader.

Not because anyone said so, but because the story shifted when we showed up. And that, I would learn again and again, is where leadership truly begins.

CHAPTER 2

REAGAN, KEMP, AND THE CALL INTO POLITICS

The morning after the Diag rally, something in me settled. It wasn't a craving for attention; it was a sense of alignment. I had stepped into a moment that mattered, and the moment had pushed back, revealing something I didn't know I'd been waiting for.

Classes resumed. Midterms approached. The Diag cycling from political battleground back to study walkway should have pulled me into normal life. But nothing felt normal anymore. The campus looked the same, yet it carried a slightly different texture — like the color palette had shifted a shade. I found myself reading between the lines of conversations, noticing the emotional currents beneath political arguments, paying attention to the cadence of speeches and the facial expressions of the people delivering them.

Reagan was the reason those details mattered.

Long before I ever stepped into a political office, he had captured my imagination. Reagan made me feel something different — something rooted in story, not statistics. He didn't talk at the country; he talked to it. He didn't overwhelm listeners with policy minutiae; he brought them into a narrative that made sense of the world around them.

Where my liberal professors layered their lectures with a haze of ideological certainty, Reagan brought clarity. Where campus speakers often sounded angry or disappointed in the country, Reagan spoke with a sense of confidence that felt both gentle and firm. His storytelling was effortless. He made America feel like a project worth participating in.

And so, wanting to get more involved in the Reagan-Bush '84 campaign, I didn't go looking for a glamorous headquarters or the strategy rooms you see in movies. I went to the Washtenaw County Republican Party office, because that's where the work actually happened.

It was hardly eye-catching, except for the signs taped to the glass windows. Inside, the air carried the scent of old carpet, photocopier toner, and a pot of coffee that had probably been reheated one time too many. The decor wasn't intentional; it was whatever furniture donors had dropped off. Donated desks. Metal folding chairs. Campaign posters from many different candidates.

This wasn't a nerve center. It was a garage band of politics. And yet it felt alive.

Volunteering meant doing the unglamorous things — knocking on doors, making phone calls, stuffing envelopes, and bundling literature into stacks that grassroots volunteers would carry into neighborhoods. The people who gathered there weren't staffers climbing ladders; they were retirees, students like me, and part-time workers who loved the country fiercely.

It was messy. It was loud. It was disorganized in a charming, chaotic way.

And it was intoxicating.

Because even in that humble little office, you could feel Reagan's story humming like a low electrical current. People didn't talk about policies first. They talked about how he made them feel. They talked about the optimism he restored, the confidence he inspired, the sense of forward motion that had settled over the country. They didn't simply support him — they believed in him.

That belief spilled into everything we did. Door-knocking wasn't just a chore; it was a mission. Phone calls weren't just about gathering data; they were invitations. Every conversation was an attempt, however small, to pull someone into the narrative that Reagan had shaped.

Working in that office was the first time I understood how a national story becomes personal action. Reagan's narrative wasn't floating above us like some abstract concept; it was directing the steps of volunteers spreading out across Ann Arbor's neighborhoods with clipboards and determination.

We were also helping Jack Lousma, the former astronaut running for U.S. Senate. Lousma's presence was so different from Reagan's that it almost felt like stepping into a different genre of political storytelling. Reagan could fill a room through a television screen. Lousma carried an understated gravity — the kind that comes from having literally seen the world from the window of a spacecraft. He didn't need theatrics. His story spoke for him.

The Washtenaw GOP office served as a local base for his campaign, too. Conversations centered on Michigan's industries, the challenges of manufacturing, the future of the state economy, and Lousma's steady, humble demeanor.

It was in those campaigns that I realized political storytelling didn't come in one flavor. Reagan brought warmth and clarity. Lousma brought discipline and integrity. Both could move people, but for different reasons. And understanding those reasons was the beginning of my education.

Then came the first time I truly heard Jack Kemp.

It wasn't in a county office or through a scratchy recording played by a volunteer trying to stir enthusiasm. It was on national television, during the Republican National Convention, as the party prepared to renominate Ronald Reagan. I had settled in to watch the lineup of speakers, expecting the usual blend of applause lines and policy nods. I wasn't looking for revelation. I certainly wasn't expecting someone new to grab hold of me.

But when Kemp stepped to the podium, something shifted.

The room changed. The energy changed. And the words that followed landed with a force I didn't realize I'd been craving.

Kemp didn't sound like a politician working through a script. He sounded like a man carrying fire. His words came fast and certain, charged with the belief that economic and political freedom formed the engine of human dignity. He spoke of growth as if it were breath itself, and of America as a force meant to lift the world.

He talked about democracy, enterprise, and the American idea with the crisp urgency of someone who knew the stakes and refused to waste a syllable. It wasn't a speech. It was a mission spoken out loud.

At the time, I had no idea Kemp had already electrified the Republican convention four years earlier. I hadn't seen that speech yet. But in 1984, sitting in front of that television, I was meeting him with fresh eyes.

I remember leaning forward without realizing it. Reagan made me feel proud of the moment I was living in. Kemp made me feel eager for the one that was coming next.

Where Reagan painted landscapes, Kemp built engines. He wasn't reflecting the era; he was pointing toward the future.

I watched the room respond to him — the applause swelling, the delegates rising, the camera panning across faces mirroring the same spark I felt. The country didn't just need Reagan's optimism; it needed someone who could carry that optimism into new territory. And in Kemp, I saw the next chapter.

By the time he finished, I knew it with absolute clarity: this was the man I wanted to succeed Ronald Reagan. This was my guy.

In Kemp, I discovered a new kind of political storytelling — one that fused head and heart so seamlessly that people didn't have to choose between reason and emotion. He offered both. And he offered them with joy.

It was the first moment I understood how a single voice, tethered to a clear and compelling narrative, could pull an entire movement into motion. Between Reagan's warmth, Lousma's steadiness, and Kemp's fire, a pattern began to form in my mind. They were all very different men, but they shared something fundamental:

They understood that leadership wasn't about explaining the world. It was about shaping the story people used to understand it.

Volunteering for the county party taught me the mechanics — how to make a list, how to read a precinct, how to persuade a single undecided voter in a conversation that lasted under a minute. But watching Reagan, Kemp, and Lousma taught me something deeper: politics was storytelling under pressure. It was narrative with consequences. It was persuasion in the open field.

Campaigns had a rhythm — rallies that felt like concerts, door-knocking that felt like reconnaissance, late nights around tables covered in maps that felt like strategy scenes from a political thriller. And I loved all of it. I loved the movement, the sense of momentum, the small victories that built toward larger ones.

Every rally felt like a scene from a film. Every volunteer night felt like a sequence in which minor characters play essential roles. Every speech felt like a plot point.

I wasn't analyzing politics anymore; I was living inside its story.

And living inside that story revealed the leadership insight I didn't yet have the vocabulary to articulate:

People don't follow data. They follow the story that makes the most sense of the moment they're living in.

Reagan gave the country a story of possibility.

Kemp gave America a story of empowerment.

Lousma gave Michigan a story of service and integrity.

Watching them didn't just inspire me. It taught me how influence actually works.

Leadership begins when you give people a narrative that helps them understand where they are, why it matters, and what comes next.

I didn't know it yet, but the road I had stepped onto — the rallies, the county offices, the late nights with phone lists — was drawing me toward a future where stories would become the core of everything I touched.

CHAPTER 3

THE MOTORCADE: CLARITY BEFORE ACTION

The first thing that struck me about the building was how ordinary it looked. You don't expect "ordinary" when the President of the United States is scheduled to arrive in a city. You expect checkpoints, security cordons, maybe an aura of theatrical importance. But when I pushed through the glass doors of the downtown Detroit facility and followed a hand-lettered sign taped to a pillar — Volunteer Driver Briefing — the hallways felt like they could have belonged to any municipal office.

It didn't matter. My pulse was already ten beats faster than usual.

A few days earlier, the President of our College Republican Chapter asked me if I'd like to drive in the motorcade for the President's visit. I signed up immediately. This wasn't a ride-along or a shuttle assignment. It was proximity to a moment. It was a chance to be part of the choreography that moves a President from one place to another. I had no idea what that truly meant, but I knew it mattered.

When I stepped into the briefing room, the contrast between the banality of the space and the significance of the event sharpened everything. The room smelled faintly of new carpet. Folding chairs were arranged in neat rows. People had already begun to gather — some older volunteers, others my age, looking both thrilled and uncertain.

Then the door opened, and the atmosphere shifted.

The man who entered didn't announce himself. He didn't need to. His presence rearranged the room. There was nothing flamboyant about him, nothing that tried to command attention, yet attention followed him naturally. He carried the kind of poise that only comes from responsibility tested countless times.

He waited until the room settled completely, then introduced himself. When he spoke, his voice was steady and measured, with the clarity of someone who understands how easily confusion becomes danger. He was Secret Service, through and through.

"This is the route."

He traced the line with a practiced gesture, stopping at each intersection. As he described the formation and pacing, the mundane conference room began to feel like the control center of something far larger. What had felt like volunteering suddenly felt like duty.

"You maintain spacing. You do not drift. You do not improvise."

He didn't speak these directives like threats. He delivered them as facts — anchors that would hold the entire formation steady.

Then came the line that stayed with me long after the briefing ended.

"If your vehicle experiences any issue — a stall, a blown tire, anything — you pull onto the shoulder immediately. Do not slow the motorcade. We will return for you."

He moved on without emphasizing it, but the weight of it lingered. The instruction wasn't just protocol; it carried a deeper message. Your role matters. Your errors have consequences. And if something happens, you will not be abandoned — but neither will the mission stop for you.

He continued outlining contingencies and communication procedures. Every word was designed to remove ambiguity. There was no inspirational rhetoric or emotional appeals. He wasn't there to motivate us; he was there to equip us with a clear frame so the actual moment could unfold without hesitation.

When the briefing ended, we stood and walked out with the quietness of individuals who had been entrusted with something important. That clarity shaped the air around us. It changed how we carried ourselves.

That clarity stayed with me the next morning when I arrived on the private tarmac at Detroit Metro Airport.

The sky was low and gray, and the wind had the bite of early fall. But what caught my attention wasn't the weather — it was the scene unfolding across the pavement. A line of station wagons stretched along the tarmac, hoods open, being inspected by bomb-sniffing dogs weaving methodically between them. Agents knelt by hinges, checked floor panels, ran gloved hands along edges I hadn't even noticed existed.

It was a quiet, intense rhythm of preparation.

Then, at the far end of the tarmac, I saw it — the presidential limousine. The 1983 Cadillac Fleetwood, nicknamed "Stagecoach," was broad and imposing even at a distance. The agent from the day before waved us over. We got to see the limo and follow car up close. Through the limo window, we could see the automatic weapon lying on the seat. The chase car had compartments in the doors with additional weapons. This was a stark reminder that this wasn't symbolic work. Every detail mattered.

The world seemed to quiet itself even further as the low rumble began — subtle at first, then growing into a physical vibration that crawled through the soles of my shoes.

Air Force One had landed and was taxiing our way.

I had seen the aircraft on television countless times, but nothing compares to being near it. The sound doesn't just fill your ears; it settles into your chest. The blue-and-white fuselage is awe-inspiring.

Seemingly as soon as the plane came to a full stop, a swarm of reporters spilled out the rear stairs and sprinted toward the front. They had been on the plane with Reagan minutes earlier, yet here they were running full-speed across the tarmac so they could stand in front of cameras and shout questions the moment he reappeared. It was absurd and theatrical and yet somehow perfectly normal in their world.

I took my spot in the motorcade, slid behind the wheel, adjusted the mirrors, and steadied my hands on the steering wheel. The car was soon filled with reporters and cameramen. When the signal came, the formation began to move.

The private runway opened into the highway, and for the first time in my life, I experienced what it felt like to drive in a world momentarily cleared of ordinary concerns. The entire stretch of freeway had been shut down. No cars merging. Just forward motion, dictated by the steady pulse of the lead vehicle's brake lights.

My station wagon's rear liftgate had been left open, as instructed. I assumed it was for ease of loading the camera gear. I learned otherwise when I caught sight of two legs dangling in my rearview mirror. A network cameraman had climbed out the back and was filming from the open doorway, bracing himself against the wind as we cruised at highway speed. One wrong tap on the brake pedal and he'd become a headline. So I kept my movements smooth and deliberate.

Then the atmosphere shifted. The radio crackled. Something spotted near an upcoming overpass. The formation slowed. The world seemed to narrow as we approached the concrete. My grip tightened on the steering wheel, but my mind was calm.

And then, just as we crested the overpass, a military helicopter rose from behind it — slow, controlled, authoritative. It was a straight-out-of-Hollywood moment and reminded me of *Blue Thunder*, the movie that had come out the previous year.

The helicopter rose with steady, almost effortless control, its movement so precise it felt rehearsed, though nothing about the moment was theatrical. It had visually checked the area. All clear.

At the time, my focus was simple: keep formation, keep the pace steady, don't tap the brakes with a cameraman hanging six feet behind me. The adrenaline kept everything sharp, and yet the moment passed without any grand personal epiphany. I was too busy doing the job to interpret it.

The understanding came later.

Years afterward — after campaigns, after crises, after leading teams through moments that required calm thinking and clear direction — I found myself looking back on that day with a new frame of reference. And in the rearview mirror of memory, the meaning came into focus.

Leadership moves like a motorcade.

Leadership moves like a motorcade. The visible part draws attention. The hidden formation makes everything possible.

People tend to notice the obvious part — the limousine gliding down the highway, the symbolic center of attention — yet the limo isn't what makes the movement possible. Its presence depends entirely on the formation surrounding it, on the unseen layers of discipline and preparation that keep it protected and on course.

The same dynamic exists in every form of leadership. Most people remember the speech, not the hours of preparation that allow the message to land. They see the person at the front of the room, but not the choices, sacrifices, and details that created the moment of clarity behind them. They respond to the leader, unaware of the story holding the team together.

Looking back, I can see the structure beneath everything that happened that day — the briefing, the route, the timing, the radios, the contingency plans, the coordination between ground and air. All of it formed the narrative that allowed the motorcade to move with purpose.

Leadership works the same way.

The visible part draws attention.

The hidden formation makes everything possible.

That day on I-94 didn't teach me the lesson in words. It engraved the experience. The understanding came later, when I had lived enough leadership moments to recognize the pattern.

Leadership moves like a motorcade. And the story established before anyone moves is what keeps the whole formation together.

LEADERSHIP PRINCIPLE: CLARITY BEFORE ACTION

Looking back, the Detroit motorcade had shown me something I'd never seen so clearly before: that clarity is not a decoration. It is the structure underneath everything — momentum, confidence, movement, trust. It is the invisible frame that allows people to act without hesitation.

But it took two very different rallies, just weeks later, for that lesson to settle into something permanent.

The first was on November 1, 1984, in the vast asphalt expanse of the Sears Lincoln Park shopping center. Mike and I arrived early with a group of friends, eager to stay as close to the action as possible. At first glance, the space looked rough and ordinary. A shopping-center lot in late autumn isn't a natural stage for a president. But the moment we stepped inside the perimeter, it was clear the Secret Service had already rewritten the atmosphere.

Eighteen-wheel tractor-trailers had been arranged into walls, turning a parking lot into a temporary arena. Their presence concentrated the space, making the air feel charged even before the crowd gathered. You could sense the subtle tension that comes from thousands of people sharing a common expectation. On the roofs of the trailers, sharpshooters paced with steady discipline, scanning the horizon with a focus that quieted every distraction.

Mike and I got separated from our friends as the crowd swelled. The afternoon moved toward evening. People pressed forward in waves, nudging Mike and me closer to the stage when one of Reagan's team removed a barrier and ushered us in. We pressed forward with the crowd right to the front — not more than twenty feet from where President Reagan would soon be standing.

When Reagan finally stepped through the wings and into view, the atmosphere didn't just erupt; it rose. As if the space itself had been waiting for the moment to arrive. As if everything had been arranged so that thousands of strangers would move together with a single understanding.

I recognize the echo of what the motorcade had already taught me: clarity is what aligns people long before the leader appears.

Fresh off the excitement of the Lincoln Park event, the next morning, Mike and I drove north to Saginaw for Reagan's airport rally at Tri-City Airport. I had expected a windswept outdoor tarmac like other airport events I'd seen. Instead, the moment we arrived, it was clear this rally had been designed with a very different energy in mind.

The stage wasn't outside at all — it was inside Hangar 5, framed by a large blue backdrop that rose almost to the ceiling. Stretching across it was a crisp banner emblazoned with a welcome for President Reagan. Red, white, and blue bunting lined the front of the stage, turning the industrial hangar into something that felt unexpectedly warm and ceremonial.

The crowd was enormous — far larger than the space was built to hold. People filled every inch of the hangar floor, shoulder to shoulder, forming a sea of jackets, signs, and breath visible in the cold November air. The hangar doors had been rolled open to accommodate overflow, and hundreds more stood outside on the tarmac, craning for a view, the cold wind snapping at their coats.

And there, behind the crowd, sat Air Force One — gleaming, enormous, unmistakable.

Its presence functioned as both backdrop and symbol, anchoring the rally with a kind of authority a campaign stage can't manufacture. Every so often, someone near us would glance over their shoulder, as if needing to confirm that the President's aircraft — this massive, iconic blue-and-white silhouette — was truly sitting right there.

Inside the hangar, you could feel a very specific kind of anticipation. The sound of conversation bounced off the metal walls and carried outward, spilling into the tarmac.

The moment Reagan appeared at the side of the stage, the reaction felt almost seismic. It wasn't a sudden explosion like an outdoor rally. It was a rising wave of sound compressed inside steel walls, carrying outward into the open air and over the tarmac where the overflow crowd erupted in response.

Even from our position in the hangar, you could feel the atmosphere tighten into focus. The blue backdrop framed him. The bunting softened the harsh industrial environment. The crowd's attention snapped forward with unified force. And behind all of us, Air Force One sat unmoving — a reminder of the scale of the moment, the weight of the office, and the clarity of the story being told long before Reagan delivered a word.

Everything about that rally — the staging, the visuals, the proximity, the presence of the aircraft — was arranged to create a shared understanding before Reagan ever stepped to the microphone.

It was a different environment from Lincoln Park. A different mood. A different kind of pressure in the air. But the same principle pulsed through every moment:

The story had been framed before anyone arrived. And that framing created the clarity that made the moment work.

Only with time did I recognize how these moments prepared me for the world I would later enter — campaigns, crisis moments, creative environments, leadership roles where people often needed direction but rarely said so out loud. You can feel when clarity is present. You can feel when it's missing. It changes the air in the room. It changes the way people stand, the way they react, the way they absorb information.

Leaders often assume clarity happens when they speak. In truth, clarity happens before they speak. It happens in the expectations they set. The tone they establish. The frame they create. The way they help people understand what this moment is and how they fit into it.

What those final days of the 1984 campaign showed me — before I could fully articulate it — was that clarity is not about giving orders. It's about shaping understanding. It's about building a frame strong enough that people can step inside and know what to do without needing to be told twice.

Clarity is the beginning of leadership.

It is the condition that allows everything else to work.

And it took a motorcade, a shopping-center rally, and a cold airport tarmac for me to finally see it.

CLARITY HOLDS THE FORMATION

There are moments in leadership when the world compresses into a single, breath-held instant — a moment when the next step matters more than the last, and the difference between confusion and confidence is measured in the blink of an eye. The motorcade taught me that long before I had language for it.

Watching the formation assemble — sweep teams, radios, agents scanning rooftops, contingencies mapped down to the second — I thought I was witnessing power. Only later did I understand I was watching something far more essential: clarity holding human beings together inside a mission none of them could carry alone.

Even now, years later, I can still picture the overpass we approached that afternoon. We didn't know if there was danger. But the team didn't guess. They didn't improvise. They didn't close their eyes and hope for the best. They acted because they were living inside a story that had already told them what the moment required. That story — the mission, the purpose, the why beneath the choreography — gave them the authority to move quickly without losing one another.

Clarity doesn't always shout. Sometimes it appears as quiet discipline. Sometimes it's a simple directive delivered calmly over a radio. Sometimes it is nothing more than shared agreement about what matters enough to do well.

What I learned from the motorcade is something I would later see in campaign war rooms, in television studios, in ministry in Ethiopia and India, and in the harder seasons of my own life: people don't follow authority — they follow meaning. Authority may coordinate movement, but only meaning coordinates trust. And trust is what keeps a formation intact when pressure rises.

In Ann Arbor, the day Mike and I stepped forward with Reagan/Bush signs and watched the crowd shift around us, I thought influence began with courage. In a way, it did. But courage without clarity can't sustain influence. Courage can spark a moment; clarity sustains the movement that follows.

And clarity isn't only something you give others. It's something you protect in yourself. Nothing disorients a team faster than a leader who doesn't know what story he is in.

That is what the motorcade taught me before I knew I was being taught: clarity is not a presentation skill, or a technique, or a communication trick. It is stewardship. Leaders are custodians of the narrative their people must inhabit. When that narrative is strong, people stand straighter. They see what needs doing. They trust one another. And they move.

When the story is unclear, people hesitate. They invent motives. They fill gaps with fear or suspicion. And the formation breaks.

Someday, you will find yourself in your own version of a motorcade moment. It may not involve sweep teams or black limousines, but the stakes will feel just as real. It will happen when the room quiets, eyes turn, and someone has to interpret the moment — and they need you to speak.

In that moment, remember the motorcade. Remember that clarity is not about giving orders. It's about giving meaning. It's about holding steady long enough for others to find their place in the story.

Leadership is less about directing the movement and more about defining the mission.

If you can give people a clear story to inhabit — one that explains why the moment matters, how their role fits, and what the next step should be — they will move with the kind of confidence that once captivated me on that Michigan highway.

Clarity is not loud. It does not demand attention. It simply removes the fog. And when the fog lifts, people know where to go.

NAME THE MOMENT

There is a moment in every organization when the hallway feels like that Detroit briefing room — plain carpet, fluorescent lights, nothing glamorous — yet the stakes have quietly risen. A project is behind schedule. A crisis is brewing. Teams are uneasy. People look toward the leader not for orders, but for meaning.

This is when confusion tries to outrun confidence. When the "formation" — a staff, a volunteer team, a ministry, a company — begins to drift because no one is sure what story they are in.

You don't need a motorcade to recognize it. You see it in the meeting where everyone talks in circles. You hear it in the same question asked three different ways. You feel it in decisions that should be simple but suddenly feel risky.

Clarity is not a speech you give. It's an atmosphere you build. And before you act, you frame the moment.

1. NAME THE MOMENT

Every motorcade briefing begins with something simple: What is this? Not logistics — meaning.

Most teams don't fall apart because they're incapable. They falter because they're guessing. So the first act of clarity is definition:

"This is a stabilization season."

"This is a reset."

"This is a high-stakes handoff."

"This is an opportunity window, and we're not wasting it."

When you name the moment in plain, human language, people stop inventing private interpretations. They settle. They exhale. They can finally stand on the same ground.

2. ESTABLISH THE MISSION FRAME

Every agent in a motorcade understands the mission before a single tire turns. That frame is what keeps the formation intact when pressure rises.

Your team needs the same anchoring clarity:

What are we doing right now?

What are we not doing?

What does "success" look like in this season — not in theory, in practice?

What is the one thing we must protect above all else?

This isn't a slogan. It's a shared definition repeated until it becomes instinct. When people know the frame, they don't need constant supervision. When they don't, every decision becomes a debate.

3. REMOVE ROLE FOG

On the tarmac that morning, nobody wondered who was driving, who was scanning rooftops, who was coordinating radios, who was clearing intersections. Ambiguity is the enemy of courage.

Clarity often sounds like ownership:

"You own this."

"You decide this."

"You communicate this."

"And if there's uncertainty, it comes to you before it goes anywhere else."

Role clarity doesn't make teams rigid. It makes them free. It stops energy from leaking through overlap, hesitation, and quiet resentment.

4. REPLACE VAGUENESS WITH EXPECTATIONS

The agent didn't tell us, "Do your best." He told us what would happen, what to do, and what mattered enough to protect. That kind of clarity isn't micromanagement. It's stewardship.

Most leaders don't realize how often they speak in fog.

Here are a few language swaps that instantly remove guesswork:

- "Keep me posted" → "Send me a status every Friday at 3 PM."
- "Let's get this done soon" → "This needs to be completed by Thursday because the next phase depends on it."
- "Just coordinate with the team" → "You two are the decision-makers. Everyone else supports."

Clarity is kindness. It respects people's time, energy, and attention by telling them what the moment requires.

A CLOSING DISCIPLINE

The motorcade wasn't impressive because anyone was heroic. It was impressive because everyone was prepared. Clarity is built before the moment arrives — in pre-briefs, rehearsed conversations, and quiet risk reviews while the room is still calm.

So here is what this requires of you when no one is watching: do the private work of definition. Write the one sentence that names the moment. Clarify what matters most. Decide what you will protect. Remove the fog from your own mind before you try to remove it from anyone else's.

Because when the moment comes — when the room quiets and eyes turn toward you — your people won't be looking for a hero. They'll be looking for someone who already knows the story they're in. Someone who can hold meaning steady long enough for the team to move as one.

Clarity is not an accessory to leadership. It is the condition that makes leadership possible — and it begins in the unseen discipline of a leader who refuses to lead from fog.

PART II

PRECISION:
THE MARINE ONE LESSON

CHAPTER 4

THE SILENT LANGUAGE OF PRECISION

Clarity sets the conditions for movement. But clarity alone isn't enough.

Once a leader has given people a story to inhabit — once the mission is defined, roles are clear, and the formation knows where it's headed — the next test arrives: Can the leader embody what they've spoken? Do their actions reinforce the narrative, or undermine it?

This is where many leaders stumble. They speak clearly but act inconsistently. They set expectations but model something different. They create narrative clarity, then blur it through imprecise execution.

And their people notice.

The second lesson I learned about leadership didn't come from a briefing room or a campaign headquarters. It came from watching a helicopter land on the South Lawn of the White House.

It was part of a Washington D.C. field experience organized by Ray Tanter, my professor at Michigan — one of the most surprising mentors I ever had. He didn't teach theory; he taught reality born from experience. Tanter had served on the National Security Council staff in the Reagan White House in 1981-82, and as a U.S. representative to arms control talks in Madrid, Helsinki, Stockholm, and Vienna.

This particular trip was designed to show us the machinery of American power from the inside.

We toured the Pentagon and the State Department, moving through corridors where the air felt heavy with the residue of decisions that had once shaped headlines. We stepped into conference rooms where national security debates had unfolded at full intensity. But the most surprising part came when we sat in on actual briefings — presentations that had been delivered to senior officials not long before. We expected complexity, nuance, layers of geopolitical shading. Instead, the briefings felt strangely simplified: a high-stakes global issue had been boiled down to something that could fit on a single page. It was disorienting. The world felt enormous and volatile, yet the explanations handed to decision-makers seemed pared down to the point of discomfort. That contrast — between the gravity of the environment and the sparseness of the messaging — lingered with all of us.

But nothing — not a single stop on that itinerary — prepared me for the moment we stepped onto the White House lawn.

After a tour of the White House, we were ushered through security and placed behind a rope line. The grass looked impossibly perfect, each blade trimmed to a uniform height, the kind of detail no one thinks about unless they're standing on ground where history routinely walks. The air felt still, almost expectant, as if the space itself understood what was about to happen.

And then the atmosphere shifted.

I didn't hear a helicopter. Not at first.

I felt it.

A low vibration crept through the air, through my chest, a frequency more than a sound. Conversations softened. Heads turned instinctively toward the tree line even before anything appeared.

Then, like a great mechanical apparition, Marine One emerged.

Hovering. Tilting. Adjusting with a grace that seemed at odds with its size.

From a distance, it looked effortless — almost slow, almost casual. But the closer it came, the more precise its movements became. The rotors cut the air with a disciplined steadiness. The entire aircraft seemed to breathe in controlled, deliberate motions.

And then it descended.

Not onto a wide concrete pad or an expansive helipad, but onto three small aluminum discs — not much larger than the wheels themselves. The pilot aligned the wheels with a precision that bordered on artistry. A clean, perfect landing, as if the helicopter were settling into a socket designed only for it.

Moments later, the door to the White House opened, and President Reagan stepped into the sunlight. He gave a small wave — warm, casual, familiar — and walked toward the helicopter with that natural stride that made everything around him seem calmer. His presence felt like a continuation of the precision we had just witnessed, as if the landing had set the tempo for everything that followed.

He boarded. The door closed, and Marine One lifted back into the sky with the same grace it had descended, tilting away from the lawn until it disappeared beyond the tree line.

And suddenly the lawn seemed still again, as if the air had exhaled.

It took me years to understand why this moment lingered so powerfully in my memory.

At twenty-one years old, I was still drawn to the visible parts of leadership — the speeches, the applause, the energy of rallies, the choreography of political moments. But that landing revealed something different, something quieter and far more enduring:

Precision tells a story. A story of discipline. A story of preparation. A story of competence so strong it doesn't need translation.

Precision tells a story. A story of discipline. A story of preparation. A story of competence so strong it doesn't need translation.

No one on that lawn needed to be told to respect that pilot. No one needed a briefing to understand the professionalism on display. The precision was the message.

Leadership, at its highest level, often works exactly this way. It communicates through consistency. It reassures through mastery. It influences through presence before it persuades through words.

Watching Marine One taught me the difference between performance and excellence. Performance seeks attention. Excellence seeks accuracy. Performance demands to be noticed. Excellence doesn't need to be. Its strength lies in its undeniability.

And this was the lesson: **Silent authority is the most trustworthy form of influence.**

The pilot never addressed us, but in the span of a few seconds, he communicated more about leadership than many people do in an entire career. Influence born from mastery requires no spotlight. It creates its own. And it shapes everyone who witnesses it.

I didn't know it then, but I would return to this principle dozens of times — when working on television shows, managing campaigns, building teams, writing briefing papers, or navigating crisis moments. Every time I felt pressure rising, every time I watched a leader falter, every time I sensed a team struggling under uncertainty, I'd think about the vibration in my chest that day — the quiet rumble that preceded a display of flawless execution.

Clarity — what the motorcade taught me — sets the conditions.

Precision — what Marine One taught me — creates the confidence.

One prepares the movement. The other sustains it. We often think leadership is about charisma. Or persuasion. Or strategy. But charisma without clarity is noise.

Persuasion without precision is manipulation. Strategy without execution is theater.

People don't follow leaders who simply speak well. They follow leaders whose actions reinforce the story they claim to tell.

Marine One did not announce its excellence. It demonstrated it. And in doing so, it revealed something I would only fully appreciate years later:

Leadership doesn't begin when you speak. It begins when your actions give people a reason to trust the sound of your voice.

Leadership doesn't begin when you speak. It begins when your actions give people a reason to trust the sound of your voice.

We felt the helicopter before we saw it.

We saw the precision before Reagan spoke.

We understood the authority before any words were exchanged.

That is the silent story great leaders tell. And it is the heartbeat of the second pillar of leadership.

Precision is communication.

CHAPTER 5

PRECISION IS COMMUNICATION

Long before I understood leadership as a discipline, I understood it as a feeling — that quiet shift inside you when you witness someone perform with such mastery that the moment becomes larger than itself. The landing of Marine One on the White House lawn was that kind of moment for me. It looked effortless, almost serene, but the serenity was the surface of something practiced, disciplined, and deeply intentional.

It was the unspoken message.

That was the moment I began to understand that precision carries its own meaning.

Effective leaders often imagine that communication happens only when they open their mouths. They focus on the speech, the presentation, the memo, the meeting. But the truth is quieter, and far more pervasive. People assign meaning long before a single sentence is spoken. They read intention in preparation. They read competence in execution. They read stability in consistency.

Even when a leader believes they are simply doing their job, the people around them are absorbing a steady stream of information: how well tasks are handled, how details are managed, how promises are kept. All of this tells a story about whether the leader is someone worth following.

Precision doesn't require perfection. It requires respect — for the craft, for the people depending on you, and for the moment you've been trusted to carry.

That Marine One landing was a brief event, barely long enough to register on a clock. Yet it revealed everything about the standards held behind the scenes. I didn't think about the pilot's training hours, or the years of experience, or the intense scrutiny required to earn a place in the cockpit of the presidential helicopter. What I absorbed — intuitively, immediately — was the commitment that had shaped those things. Commitment, in its purest form, becomes visible.

The absence of precision carries a message just as quickly. When tasks are rushed, when deadlines slide, when the small things are treated carelessly, people don't merely notice the lapse; they feel it. Doubt creeps in. Confidence weakens. Teams become hesitant, unsure when the next misstep will appear. Without ever intending to, the leader has created a secondary narrative, one that fights against the goals they're trying to advance.

In leadership, the gap between intention and perception is rarely neutral. People don't see the reasons behind inconsistency. They only experience the results.

The pilot did not teach a class that day — no guidelines on leadership. Yet he delivered one of the clearest lessons of my life: precision steadies the people who are watching. It offers them a place to anchor their trust. It signals reliability without having to declare it. And it heightens the impact of the leader's words because the foundation beneath them feels solid.

When President Reagan walked across the lawn, waving to our group, the moment had already been framed. The pilot had set the tone. Reagan's presence added to it, but the atmosphere of competence was established before he appeared. Leadership isn't always about being the one in front. It's often shaped by the unseen disciplines of the people who make the moment possible.

I've watched organizations over the years that struggled, not because they lacked talent or resources, but because precision had been treated as an accessory rather than a core part of the culture. The result was a story no one intended to tell — a story of drift, ambiguity, and lowered expectations. Teams flounder when they cannot sense steadiness above them.

I've also seen the opposite. A leader who prepares thoroughly, who honors commitments, and who treats details with care becomes a source of confidence even before speaking. People may not articulate why they trust that person, but they feel the difference. Structure appears where there had been confusion. Decisions come easier. Communication travels farther because the leader has already spoken volumes through behavior.

Marine One didn't leave me with an inspirational quote or an emotional surge. It left me with a standard. The lesson was simple, but it carried depth that I would grow into over the years:

How you execute tells the story that people will believe.

How you execute tells the story that people will believe.

Precision is not pomp. It's not performance. It's quiet integrity expressed through action. When leaders embrace that standard, they communicate reliability at a level that words cannot reach.

That day, as the helicopter lifted away with the same grace it had landed, I understood something that had been unfolding throughout my life without me naming it. Precision is one of the most persuasive forms of communication because it reaches people on a level beneath rhetoric. It speaks to their need for steadiness. It tells them the leader's hand is trustworthy. It turns uncertainty into confidence, and confidence into unity.

A leader can talk about excellence all day long.

But only precision proves it.

MORALE AS A CONSEQUENCE OF PRECISION

When I was thirteen, standing in that television studio with a headset clamped to my ears, I didn't need anyone to explain leadership to me. I felt it. The director's panic moved through the room like static. His frustration didn't just signal a mistake — it created instability. Everyone felt it. Everyone adjusted to it. Chaos, I learned early, is contagious.

Years later, watching the Marine One pilot descend onto three aluminum plates, I witnessed the opposite effect. His calm precision didn't inspire through words. It inspired through steadiness. The Secret Service agents and military personnel around him moved with confidence because the tone had already been set. He didn't raise morale with encouragement. He stabilized it with execution.

That's when it became clear to me: leaders don't just communicate direction — they set the emotional temperature of the room. And they do it whether they intend to or not.

A leader's internal state becomes the team's external reality.

Anxious leaders create hesitant teams.

Scattered leaders create reactive ones.

Steady leaders create confidence by example.

This is why precision matters beyond performance. When leaders prepare thoroughly, honor commitments, and execute with discipline, they aren't just managing tasks. They are quietly restoring trust. Morale rises not because someone demanded it, but because people feel safe enough to give their best again.

I've watched leaders inherit teams already worn thin — by broken promises, constant pivots, and years of inconsistency. In those moments, speeches don't help. Vision statements don't heal fatigue. What changes the atmosphere is something far less dramatic: a pattern of steadiness. Small decisions handled well. Problems addressed without panic. Follow-through that doesn't depend on applause.

Demoralized teams don't need hype. They need proof. Proof that chaos won't be passed downstream. Proof that today won't feel like yesterday. Proof that the person leading them can be trusted to carry pressure without transferring it.

Morale doesn't recover all at once. It returns quietly — the moment people stop bracing for the next misstep. The moment they realize the leader will show up the same way tomorrow as they did today. The moment precision replaces unpredictability.

Marine One didn't lift morale with a speech. It didn't need to. Its precision told a better story — one of steadiness, competence, and trust. That is how confidence is built. Not in grand gestures, but in the quiet consistency that allows people to breathe again.

A leader can talk about excellence all day long.

But only precision convinces people it's real.

CHAPTER 6

FORKLIFTS AND SHOPPING MALLS

By 1988, I had already lived a lifetime's worth of miles inside the Jack Kemp for President campaign. I had fought to elect delegates in Michigan and then packed my life into a car and followed the campaign west for the Iowa caucuses. I knew the rhythm of field offices, the slang of strategists, and the exhaustion that settles into a campaign staffer's bones around the tenth straight month of seven-day weeks.

So when our team converged on Minneapolis-Saint Paul, I arrived with the easy familiarity of someone who understood the choreography. Another state. Another scramble for delegates. Another attempt to translate Kemp's ideas into momentum.

And for me, Jack Kemp was worth that effort.

I admired him long before I worked for him. He had the optimism of Reagan but carried it differently. Reagan lifted a room through story. Kemp lifted a room through energy — ideas crackling like live wires, economics delivered with such passion that you could forget he was talking about marginal tax rates or gold standards. He had the unusual ability to connect policy to dignity, and I loved that about him.

Working for him wasn't an obligation; it felt like a privilege.

There was also something else about Jack that people didn't always expect.

One night, after a long day of campaigning, a few of us were sitting around dinner — exhausted in that familiar, bone-deep way campaigns produce. Jack was seated next to me.

He leaned over and asked casually, "So, did you catch the game last night?"

I laughed. "Are you kidding? I was working... for you."

He looked back at me, grinning. "Working? During Monday Night Football?" He shook his head. "That's un-American."

Jack Kemp had been a quarterback long before he was elected to Congress. Football wasn't a prop to him. It was part of how he saw the world — teamwork, discipline, execution under pressure. And it showed, even when the cameras weren't around. That understanding of who Jack was, and who he wasn't, would matter more than we realized once the campaign arrived in Minnesota.

OUTSIDERS ADVANCING A CITY WE'D NEVER SEEN

Minnesota brought its own cast of characters, but the dynamic was familiar: Washington-based senior staff with impeccable resumes but little patience for mornings before sunrise, regional organizers who knew the terrain better than anyone gave them credit for, and local political allies who insisted their part of the schedule was absolutely essential.

Before we could execute anything, though, we had to set the stage. The local team handed the advance assignment to me and my colleague, who had been shoulder-to-shoulder with me through the endless grind of precinct organizing, delegate wrangling, and every unpredictable twist of the Michigan and Iowa caucuses. Handing the advance to us instead of the locals was almost comical. Neither of us had ever been to Minneapolis or even to Minnesota. We didn't know the streets, didn't know the landmarks, didn't know the rhythms of the city.

Yet there we were, sitting in our car holding a sheet of handwritten notes someone had ripped from a legal pad: "Radio station — corner of 3rd and 5th." That was all the direction we got.

We opened the Thomas Brothers map, found the intersection, and drove to the spot. It led us to a construction zone and a few empty buildings. No tower. No station. No sign we were anywhere close.

We checked the map again and that's when we realized that Minneapolis wasn't arranged like Ann Arbor, Detroit, or any Midwestern city we had ever navigated. Minneapolis is built on a hard grid. Streets run east-west. Avenues run north-south. And every single one is assigned a quadrant — NE, NW, SE, SW. A pairing like "3rd and 5th" isn't one place. It's several.

Eventually, after scanning the map like people trying to decipher a foreign subway system, we took a guess, followed a hunch, and turned into a different quadrant of the city. And there it was: a radio tower rising above the skyline like we'd known what we were doing all along.

Once we hit that first mark, the rest of the advance work fell into place. We confirmed the church entrance, checked the timing at the mall, and traced the route to the UPS facility with a precision that belied the chaos of our morning.

By the time Jack Kemp stepped into the caravan the next day, the entire schedule unfolded with smooth confidence — because precision, when done well, becomes invisible.

A BATTLE OVER DAWN

The itinerary included four stops: a radio interview, a church service, a mall appearance, and the event at the center of a quiet but persistent quarrel — an early-morning visit to a UPS facility during shift change.

The local Congressman had pushed hard for that stop. He believed it mattered, not symbolically but substantively. These were working men and women. People who understood sweat, schedule, and the grind of daily life. They were exactly the kind of people Kemp resonated with.

The Washington team didn't see it that way. They saw the hour. They saw the fatigue. They saw the potential for a lackluster turnout.

The fight wasn't dramatic, but the resistance was steady. Was it really worth waking everyone at dawn? Would a handful of workers be enough to justify the disruption? Would anyone care?

I argued that the stop was important. Jack belonged in that environment. He didn't need lighting cues or podiums. He needed real conversations with real people. The UPS facility stayed on the schedule.

THE FORKLIFT

We arrived while the sky was still indigo — a sharp, cold Minnesota morning. The air smelled faintly of diesel and wet asphalt. Delivery trucks lined the yard. Workers filtered in with the steady rhythm of people beginning a morning routine they could perform in their sleep.

Jack strode into that environment like he had been born for it. He talked with the workers, asked questions, and listened. Someone offered him a chance to drive a forklift, and he didn't hesitate. There was no political calculation in it. It was pure connection.

A local news crew captured the moment. Hours later, the footage hit CNN Headline News. Jack Kemp, candidate for President, driving a forklift.

It wasn't a staged stunt or a forced photo op. It was a moment that felt true.

And because it was true, it ran all day — segment after segment, hour after hour — carrying the quiet authority of authenticity.

THE MALL WALK

Later that day, we reached the mall. Jeff Kemp — Jack's son and quarterback for the Seattle Seahawks — had joined us.

Our press secretary spotted what he thought might be a perfect visual. He bought a football from the sporting goods store, and the plan was simple: let Jack and Jeff toss it casually through the mall — father and son, candidate and quarterback — something warm, spontaneous, relatable.

We all agreed. It felt like the kind of moment that could land beautifully on the evening news.

But the camera has a way of revealing when a story rings hollow.

The crowd watched with amusement. Kids followed Jeff's throws with wide eyes. Parents lingered at the edges. Jeff's passes cracked through the air with the kind of velocity only an NFL arm delivers. It was fun, undeniably so. And in another context, it might have been perfect.

But it didn't belong to Kemp.

The morning at UPS had been different — grounded, gritty, authentic. Jack talking with workers, riding the forklift, laughing with people who lived the economic struggles he fought for. That wasn't staged. That was who he was.

The mall moment, though charming, carried no weight. It was clever. It just wasn't true in the way the forklift was true.

And when the moment doesn't match the leader, the camera senses it long before the audience does.

> When the moment doesn't match the leader, the camera senses it long before the audience does.

WHAT PRECISION REALLY MEANS

Minnesota taught me that precision isn't just about avoiding mistakes. It's about aligning action with identity. A forklift at dawn fit Jack Kemp like a glove. A football in a shopping mall did not.

The world sees the difference.

One moment echoed across national coverage. The other evaporated the second Jack walked out of the building.

Leadership doesn't require spectacle. It requires truth presented with clarity. Precision is not polish. It's coherence.

Precision is not polish. It's coherence.

And in Minnesota, I learned that the best visuals aren't created. They're revealed when the right leader meets the right moment with the right purpose.

CRASHING THE VICE PRESIDENT'S RALLY

Before I ever set foot in Minnesota, before the forklift, before the mall walk and the debate over dawn, I witnessed something in Iowa that redefined what boldness looked like on a campaign trail. It came not from Jack Kemp or George Bush or Bob Dole, but from someone most voters barely remembered — Pierre "Pete" du Pont.

If you weren't politically attuned in the 1980s, du Pont might seem like a footnote. He shouldn't be. He was a former governor of Delaware, heir to the sprawling du Pont fortune, the kind of man whose ideas were sharp and radical in the best way — school choice, economic modernization, entitlement reform long before it was fashionable. He was earnest, intelligent, unfailingly polite, and absolutely fearless in a way that didn't draw attention to itself until the moment arrived.

And in Iowa, the moment arrived.

It happened at a rally for Vice President Bush — one of those large, choreographed caucus events where the room is packed to the rafters, music pumping, signs bobbing, staffers weaving through the crowd with headsets and clipboards, waiting for the motorcade to pull up outside. Bush was running a machine campaign. His operation was crisp, professional, and unyieldingly disciplined. Everything had a purpose. Everything had a place.

Which made what happened next even more astonishing.

A murmur started at the back of the hall. At first, it sounded like a simple ripple of movement — people shifting to make space, heads turning, a line of sight opening. The way crowds adjust when something unexpected is happening. But this wasn't anxiety. It was curiosity. And then surprise.

Pete du Pont was walking through the room.

He was working the crowd — shaking hands, smiling, passing out brochures to voters who were very clearly at a Bush rally, not his.

There was no hesitation in him, no embarrassment at the impropriety of it. He wasn't trying to stage a confrontation or manufacture a headline. He was simply campaigning — inside someone else's event — as if this were the most natural thing in the world.

And the thing was… people loved it.

At first, there was confusion, then recognition, then delight. It's rare to see spontaneity in a presidential campaign. So much is choreographed, staged, and negotiated. Du Pont broke the pattern simply by being present where no one expected him. He instantly became the story in a room designed for someone else.

The Bush staff didn't know what to do. They had meticulously planned every aspect of the rally. But there's no contingency plan for a rival candidate politely shaking hands in your audience. And because he wasn't disruptive, they couldn't justify removing him. He moved through the room with the easy confidence of a man who believed he had every right to be there.

He had read the room, read the campaign, and understood exactly what would make him unforgettable that night. Boldness, delivered with such sincerity that it felt disarming rather than confrontational.

I had never seen anything like it.

It taught me that precision on a campaign trail doesn't always look like discipline or logistics or flawlessly timed visuals. Sometimes it looks like instinct. Sometimes it looks like courage. And sometimes it looks like a man walking into the strongest room his opponent has — carrying nothing more threatening than a stack of brochures and a handshake.

The moment stayed with me for years. It reframed how I viewed political storytelling: not as something delivered from a podium, but as something that can happen in the unscripted space between expectation and surprise.

It was a lesson that followed me into Minnesota — into the forklift at dawn, the mall walk, and the realization that authenticity will always outshine choreography.

Because the truth is this: Sometimes precision is planned. Sometimes it's improvised. And sometimes, as Pete du Pont proved that night in Iowa, it walks straight into the lion's den and changes the story simply by showing up.

SILENT AUTHORITY AND EARNED TRUST

Long before we learn to speak with authority, people read us. They read our habits, our preparation, our tone, our steadiness. They decide — often without saying a word — whether our voice carries weight.

That is why the Marine One moment has never left me. Not because it was dramatic, but because it clarified what communication really is. The pilot didn't persuade us with language. He persuaded us with mastery.

Precision is not perfection. It is respect — for the craft, for the people depending on you, and for the moment you've been trusted to carry. Watching that helicopter descend onto three small plates showed me that excellence doesn't announce itself. It arrives quietly, through discipline that has been practiced long before anyone is watching.

And that truth follows leaders everywhere.

In campaign headquarters, you can feel within minutes whether precision lives in the room — in how deadlines are treated, how briefing papers are handled, how schedules are protected, how details are honored or neglected. Precision is the difference between a formation that moves with confidence and a team that stumbles into avoidable crises. Most people blame the crisis. Few trace it back to the drift that came first.

I saw the same dynamic in television production. A director who walked into a studio unprepared didn't just make mistakes — he spread uncertainty. His urgency became the room's urgency. Even at thirteen, I could feel how one person's lack of discipline could rattle everyone downstream.

Marine One revealed the inverse: steadiness that teaches without speaking. Leaders underestimate how much people absorb from the smallest signals. Teams feel whether you arrive hurried or grounded. They notice whether you follow through or improvise. They sense whether your standards are real or merely aspirational. Precision isn't limited to high-security landings or international diplomacy. It lives in the fabric of everyday leadership.

And when it's missing, people feel that, too. They may not be able to name it, but they instinctively step back. Trust loosens. Energy deflates. Alignment weakens.

This is why precision must be cultivated, not demanded.

The Marine One pilot wasn't performing for us. He was simply doing what disciplined people do: honoring the responsibility in their hands. That posture communicates long before any formal message reaches the room. Consistency builds trust. Trust builds influence. Influence builds confidence. And confidence gives teams the courage to move forward together.

That day on the South Lawn, we felt competence so ingrained it looked effortless. We felt steadiness before we understood why we felt it.

And this is the principle I've carried ever since: the strongest leaders don't generate confidence at the microphone. They generate it in the hours no one sees — in preparation, in follow-through, in the unglamorous disciplines that tell people, You are safe to follow me because I have taken this seriously.

Marine One didn't just land on three aluminum plates that day. It landed on every leadership assumption I had brought with me — and replaced them with a new standard:

Precision is communication.

How you execute tells the story people will believe.

MAKE PRECISION VISIBLE

There is a moment in every organization when people stop listening to what you say and begin watching how you move. They study your habits. They notice whether you show up prepared. They absorb your tone, your steadiness, your follow-through.

Before you ever speak, they read you.

Precision is not about perfection. It's about alignment. It's the quiet way a leader tells the truth with their actions — and invites everyone else to do the same.

If you want the Marine One lesson to live inside your leadership, don't start with performance. Start with discipline.

1. DO THE UNSEEN WORK UNTIL IT SHOWS

The Marine One pilot didn't "pull off" a flawless landing. He lived inside a standard forged long before the rotors ever turned — in training runs, checklists, rehearsals, and a thousand repetitions no one witnessed.

Leadership works the same way. The meeting goes better because you reviewed the briefing before anyone arrived. The hard conversation goes cleaner because you rehearsed the truth before you delivered it. The decision earns trust because you studied the cost before you sold the vision.

Preparation is a silent promise: You are safe with me.

2. LET CONSISTENCY BECOME YOUR SIGNATURE

Marine One's landing wasn't impressive because it was dramatic. It was impressive because it was routine. Precision has power when it becomes predictable — not rigid, but reliable.

Begin meetings when you say you will. Deliver work when you promise. Repeat standards until they become culture. Create rhythms your team can depend on.

When your consistency becomes unmistakable, people stop bracing for chaos. They stop second-guessing. They start moving.

3. REFUSE THE GAP BETWEEN YOUR STORY AND YOUR BEHAVIOR

Nothing erodes trust faster than a leader whose actions contradict their narrative. If you preach accountability but miss your own deadlines, you don't have a culture problem — you have a credibility problem. If you preach calm but respond with volatility, the room won't remember your values. It will remember your temperature.

Precision is integrity in motion. It's the leader living the standard before asking others to carry it.

The camera always knows the difference between performance and truth. So does your team.

4. SHAPE THE ROOM BEFORE THE ROOM SHAPES YOU

When Marine One arrived, the atmosphere changed. People stood straighter. Conversations softened. The moment carried weight before Reagan ever appeared.

Leaders do that too — whether they mean to or not.

Your pace, your focus, your composure, your attention to detail — these are forms of communication. If you enter hurried, you teach urgency. If you enter scattered, you teach reactivity. If you enter steady, you teach confidence.

Morale doesn't rise because you announce it. It rises because your steadiness makes it possible.

A CLOSING DISCIPLINE

If you want one place to start, start small — because trust is cumulative.

Here is what this requires of you when no one is watching: keep the micro-promises that never make it into the highlight reel. Prepare before you speak. Review what you said you would review. Finish what you said you would finish. Tell the truth in the small places where it would be easier to cut the corner and no one would ever know.

Document decisions clearly. Remove clutter from communication. Treat people's time like it matters. Do the quiet work before the visible moment arrives.

Someday your team will face a moment when they don't need inspiration. They need steadiness. And in that moment, they won't be measuring your charisma. They'll be drawing confidence from the story your habits have been telling all along.

Precision is leadership without noise. Excellence without drama. And it is built — always — in the hours no one sees.

PART III

NARRATIVE: HOW FRAMING DECIDES THE OUTCOME

CHAPTER 7

THE LAST RANCHER

Clarity tells people where they are. Precision shows them you can be trusted. But there's a third essential element of leadership communication that determines whether you win or lose before the first move is made: the narrative frame itself.

It's not enough to be clear and precise if you're fighting on the wrong battlefield. The story you choose to tell — and the frame through which people interpret your actions — can determine outcomes more powerfully than the quality of your execution.

> The story you choose to tell — and the frame through which people interpret your actions — can determine outcomes more powerfully than the quality of your execution.

This is what the best political strategists understand instinctively: narrative framing decides the game. Get the frame right, and even setbacks can reinforce your position. Get it wrong, and victories can slip away.

I saw this lesson played out clearly in a State Assembly campaign in California. I hadn't been in the state long enough to know the back roads of the district, but I already found myself running one of the most fiercely contested Assembly races in the state. In Michigan, a campaign with thirty-five thousand dollars was considered big. In California, that wouldn't cover your yard signs and coffee. This race operated in a different universe. By Election Day, the budget had climbed past one million dollars — an almost surreal figure for a single Assembly district in 1988.

Campaigning in California didn't feel like politics. It felt like an arms race waged at street level.

Our candidate was David Knowles, a mortgage broker. David was personable and sharp. He had a firm grasp of the issues and carried himself with a quiet steadiness. He was a newcomer going up against Assemblyman Norm Waters, who had held the seat for twelve years.

And he wasn't simply running against a local incumbent. He was pushing against the entire gravitational field of California politics.

At the time, Willie Brown was Speaker of the Assembly — the most formidable political force in the state. Under his leadership, no incumbent Democrat had lost a State Assembly race in nearly twenty years. It wasn't merely unlikely that Waters would fall. History itself suggested it wasn't going to happen. People didn't talk about flipping Democratic incumbents. They talked about surviving them.

But we believed we could do it.

Our consulting team was built for a fight. Ray McNally — inventive, restless, always story-driven — shaped the creative. Richard Temple brought the discipline, the strategic rigor, the method behind the message. They handled the air war: television, radio, mail. We ran the ground game: precincts, fundraising events, volunteer mobilization, candidate forums, the countless hours of shaking hands and listening.

By election night, we felt the momentum. That's the danger of campaigns: confidence whispers to you long before the votes justify it.

Our victory party looked like the culmination of a winning effort. Governor Deukmejian was there. State Senator John Doolittle came to show his support. Donors, volunteers, local leaders — all packed shoulder to shoulder, carrying the anticipatory energy of a room poised for celebration. As the first numbers trickled in, pockets of the district broke our way. Then more. The line on the board moved, dipped, rose, dipped again — the strange heartbeat of election night.

By midnight, we were still ahead.

People hugged. Drinks flowed. Many went home expecting to wake up to good news.

But somewhere around 2 a.m., the room changed — dramatically. It wasn't a shifting tide; it was a tsunami. Richard and I stood watching as the numbers flipped.

The truth was unavoidable.

We had lost.

The margin was excruciating: 702 votes out of 172,000 cast. A fraction of a percentage point. Close enough to see victory across the chasm, far enough to know you would never reach it.

There's a specific kind of silence that follows a loss like that. It isn't dramatic. It's hollow. A kind of emotional aftershock that makes your mind reassemble the campaign moment by moment, searching for the hinge — that one decision, one message, one knock on one door — that might have shifted the outcome.

You don't replay the whole race. You replay the pieces you can't change. The precinct you meant to revisit. The volunteer you should have listened to. The mailer you weren't sure about. The message you believed in but didn't push quite hard enough.

One of those details emerged from a mistake we hadn't discovered until it was too late.

THE MAILER THAT NEVER MOVED

Throughout the campaign, we relied heavily on direct mail — a critical component in the pre-digital era. We were fortunate to have a staffer, Donn Zea, who treated mail tracking with the seriousness of a military operation. Donn built relationships with postmasters across our seven-county district. He knew which distribution centers moved efficiently, which needed additional prompting, and which required near-constant oversight. When a mailer went out, he was on the phone with the post office every step of the way, ensuring that nothing stalled.

But in the final weeks — when the timing of every message becomes absolutely crucial — legislative leadership reassigned Donn to assist on another high-priority race elsewhere in the state. It was a decision made with the broader battlefield in mind, but it removed the one person who monitored an essential part of our operation.

On Election Day, while our volunteers were working precincts and we were executing get-out-the-vote efforts, my phone rang. The caller was the postmaster from the main West Sacramento facility.

His tone was polite but matter-of-fact.

"Are you aware that you've got a mailer that's been sitting on our dock for the last couple of days?"

I wasn't aware.

It felt like the floor dropped out from beneath me.

This wasn't an ordinary mailer. It was a powerful letter from Governor George Deukmejian — strongly worded, direct, and influential. It was precisely the kind of message that could make a difference in the final days of a tight race.

But it never reached the voters.

The problem, as the postmaster explained, was simple: there hadn't been quite enough money in the postage account to cover the mailing. Not a dramatic shortfall — just enough to cause the trays to be set aside awaiting further instruction. Without Donn shepherding the process, no one caught it.

And so the mailer sat.

Would it have changed the outcome? In a race decided by 702 votes, it's impossible not to wonder. But campaigns rarely hinge on one moment. More often, they are shaped by the accumulation of small, preventable errors that surface only when it's too late to do anything about them.

That night, as I looked at the final margins, the Deukmejian letter was one of the moments that replayed most clearly in my mind.

THE REMATCH — AND AN ARMY OF VOLUNTEERS

Campaigns are cyclical, and two years later, we were back — same district, same candidate, same opponent. And this time, the lesson wasn't about mail. It was about narrative.

By 1990, the political environment had shifted. State resources were redirected south to protect another vulnerable seat. Support we had received in the prior cycle wasn't returning. We were outspent five to one and operating with a smaller staff.

But we were not alone.

The local California Republican Assembly threw itself into the race with remarkable energy. They worked the church networks, rallied activists, and built a volunteer force that extended our reach far beyond what our budget could have supported. Their contribution wasn't flashy, but it was essential. In an underfunded campaign, they provided the organizational backbone that kept us competitive.

Their work mattered. And it would matter even more as the narrative battle unfolded.

"B.S."

Late in the 1988 race, our opponent, Norm Waters, had been caught on camera at a public debate dismissing the value of prayer and church attendance, calling it "B.S." He said it plainly, and it was caught on tape. The moment nearly cost him his seat.

The clip was memorable, jarring, and deeply at odds with the values of a district that took matters of faith seriously. And unlike some political missteps, this one wasn't ambiguous. There was no "out of context," no subtle nuance. He had said what he said.

Heading into the 1990 race, we knew that clip would be our strongest asset. His campaign knew it too. Under normal circumstances, the obvious strategy for an incumbent would be to deny, to contextualize, or to sidestep the moment.

His campaign manager, who was both disciplined and unnervingly perceptive, understood something most people overlook: you don't always defeat an attack by responding to it. Sometimes the best defense is to rewrite the story before the attack arrives.

That's where the brilliance of their strategy revealed itself.

THE REFRAME

Rather than denying the comment up front, they reframed it by reshaping Waters' identity. Their campaign rolled out a theme branding him as "The Last Rancher" — a regular, rough-edged, straight-talking local who wasn't polished, rehearsed, or steeped in political theater. He wasn't the kind of man who measured his words through focus groups. He spoke plainly because that's what ranchers do.

It was a classic example of preemptive narrative construction. By leaning into his unfiltered persona, they could reframe the "B.S." comment as nothing more than a rancher being a rancher. A little blunt, a little impulsive, but honest. In that frame, the comment wasn't a moral indictment — it was simply part of the texture of an authentic life.

That frame sanded the rough edges off a moment that could otherwise cut sharply. It built a shield around the flaw by embedding it inside a broader, favorable story.

Had nothing else changed, that frame might have held.

But frames are delicate. They rely on emotional coherence. When something disrupts the emotional logic of a narrative, that story can collapse quickly. And that disruption came from a place none of us expected.

THE PARODY THAT CRACKED THE FRAME

An independent group, Gun Owners of California, released a parody ad mocking "The Last Rancher" theme. The ad was created by Wayne Johnson, one of the most creative political minds in California, and someone with whom I would go on to form a long friendship and working relationship.

"The Last Rancher" ad wasn't mean-spirited; it was clever, playful, and hilariously accurate. It exaggerated the rancher persona just enough to make it look manufactured. Instead of reinforcing authenticity, it exposed the orchestration behind it.

In a single stroke, the parody made voters question the sincerity of the frame. Was Waters really the unscripted, authentic figure the campaign portrayed? Or was the entire identity a piece of campaign branding dressed up in denim?

The power of parody is that it punctures with a smile, not a sword. The ad made the story around Waters feel less believable. And once voters begin to doubt the frame, the frame no longer protects.

When we aired our own commercial — the one with the actual footage of Waters dismissing prayer as "B.S." — the counterattack never came. The parody had pre-softened the ground. The frame his team had carefully built no longer offered the protection they needed. Our message didn't collide with a fortified wall; it landed in a space where voters were already reconsidering what they thought they knew. And with that, the race shifted.

THE VICTORY

On Election Day, we won by roughly 1,500 votes. We had been outspent five to one. We had a fraction of the manpower. We mailed one campaign piece in a race that would normally demand dozens. We were the underdog in every measurable category.

But we won.

It was also the first time in twenty years that an incumbent Democrat in the state had been defeated. And while that victory certainly helped my own career, the more significant takeaway was not political — it was psychological.

The campaign taught me a truth that has shaped every leadership conversation I've had since:

The outcome didn't turn on money, or staff, or even the message. It turned on the frame.

The outcome didn't turn on money, or staff, or even the message. It turned on the frame.

When the frame around our opponent was strong, our attack likely would have faltered. When his frame cracked, our attack landed. When the narrative made sense, voters followed it. When the narrative shifted, so did their judgment.

People do not make decisions by sorting through data. They make decisions by organizing data inside a story that feels true.

This was as real in that California Assembly race as it is in business, nonprofits, civic leadership, and every environment where people must interpret complexity. Facts matter, but they matter only after they have been placed inside a frame.

Understanding that distinction — recognizing the difference between information and interpretation — changes how you lead. It changes how you communicate. It changes how you resolve conflict and how you guide people through uncertainty.

In 1990, we didn't just win a political campaign.

We witnessed, up close, how narratives decide outcomes long before the final message is delivered.

CHAPTER 8

BLANK SPACES

There are campaigns that fall apart because of strategy, or money, or timing. And then there are campaigns that fall apart for reasons no one wants to admit — because the story itself wasn't honest.

I learned that lesson the hard way.

I was helping run a congressional campaign for a candidate who seemed, in every tangible way, built for the moment. He was a self-made millionaire, sharp as a razor, personable in every room he entered, and willing to fund his own run. We had a budget that crossed the million-dollar mark — the kind of campaign where everything hums with energy and possibility if you just execute correctly.

And we did.

Our mail hit the right issues. Our targeting was precise. Our television spots were clean and credible. Our radio ads tested well.

On paper, everything lined up.

But there was something in the candidate's biography that kept bothering me. I couldn't figure out what. It wasn't a lie — at least not on its face — but it felt incomplete, like someone had cut a paragraph out of a chapter and slid the remaining pieces together hoping no one would see the seam. Every time I read it, something inside me tightened. I asked if we could revise it. Add a little more. Clarify a few things. The campaign manager worked on it endlessly with the candidate, polishing the words, smoothing the edges, rearranging sentences.

But the same uneasy feeling stayed with me. It was as if the bio was trying too hard to sound like a story without actually being one. And in the final weeks of the campaign, the inevitable happened.

The opposition's attack ads hit — TV, radio, mail, every channel at once — all driving the same wedge into the same delicate place:

"What do we really know about this guy?"

"What's he hiding?"

There was no evidence of wrongdoing — no scandal, no paper trail they could point to. But there was a gap in his story — one we hadn't filled — and our opponents simply stepped into it and painted their version onto the empty space.

We had no answer. No counterpunch. No narrative to fight back with.

The voters felt the uncertainty long before the data showed it. And the race slipped away.

We didn't lose because of messaging or money or strategy. We lost because the story underneath the campaign wasn't aligned, and when pressure came, that fracture widened into a canyon.

That loss taught me something I didn't fully understand until years later:

If a leader leaves blanks in his own story, the world will fill them in — and never in his favor.

> If a leader leaves blanks in his own story, the world will fill them in — and never in his favor.

THE BATTLESHIP THAT WASN'T

Not every integrity test arrives as a scandal or a memo. Sometimes it's a quiet sentence you barely notice — until it detonates years later.

By the time State Senator Dick Mountjoy ran for the U.S. Senate, we had logged many miles together. He had served a term as President of the California Republican Assembly and built a long, respected career in the California Legislature.

Years earlier, when he was retiring from the legislature, I had produced a tribute video for his dinner. It was a fun project — clips of Dick doing what he did best: arguing, needling, pushing back on the floor. The script wasn't mine. His chief of staff had written it from memory, and I shaped it for the screen.

Buried inside that script sat a dormant land mine: "He served in the Korean War aboard the battleship USS Missouri…"

It sounded right. That's what everyone remembered. And at a retirement dinner, no one is pulling Navy logs. It was a tribute, not opposition research.

Years passed.

When it became clear Republicans might not field a candidate to challenge Senator Dianne Feinstein, Dick entered the race. He was a long shot with no budget, so we needed a quick way to introduce him to a statewide audience — a working-class kid who served his country, built a business, and spent decades in public service.

Someone suggested putting the old retirement video on the campaign website.

It made sense. We uploaded it and moved on. In a low-budget statewide race, you reuse everything.

Then the phone rang.

A reporter had been combing through our site and did some checking. According to the Navy logs, Dick hadn't served on the *Missouri*. He served on the USS *Bremerton*, a heavy cruiser. Same war. Same danger. But in political combat, the difference between a cruiser and the Missouri might as well be the difference between truth and deceit.

The story hit print: the challenger's official biography had misstated his military service. Feinstein's campaign pounced, suggesting the flap raised doubts about his credibility.

Inside our campaign, it felt like a sniper shot we never saw coming.

And then, in the adrenaline of those first hours, a memory surfaced — something small from the retirement dinner years earlier. When the video played, and the line about the Missouri appeared, Dick had quietly said, "I wasn't on the Missouri."

No fuss. He wasn't the type to nitpick a sentimental evening.

And in hindsight, we all let it pass. It was just a retirement video, a moment of nostalgia. No one thought to re-edit it. Years later, when we placed that same video on the campaign website, the mistake came with it — forgotten, unnoticed, waiting for precisely the wrong moment to reappear.

Remembering that made the whole thing sting more. Dick had always been straightforward — blunt, honest, allergic to embellishment. The idea that he would inflate his service record was absurd.

But intent doesn't matter once a narrative breaks loose.

We scrambled to correct the website, scrub the reference, and clarify that Dick had served honorably in Korea on the *Bremerton*. The facts weren't in dispute. Only the ship was.

It didn't matter.

The story slipped out of our hands and traveled on its own. It moved from print to chatter, from chatter to punchline. One night, Jay Leno made a joke about a Senate candidate who couldn't keep his war story straight. Even allies tried to push back, explaining why the criticism was unfair.

By then, the damage was done.

From a strategic standpoint, it was maddening. There was no lie, no embellishment, no attempt to fabricate a heroic narrative. But campaigns don't get graded on intentions. They get graded on the story you allow to stand.

In a race where we were already outspent and outgunned, we now carried a frame we never chose: If he's wrong about his own ship, what else is he wrong about?

Mountjoy was always a long shot. Beating the Feinstein machine would have required a miracle. But this still cut deep. Dick Mountjoy, a man whose integrity was beyond question, had his reputation skewered on national television.

I carried a sharp lesson out of that race: in high-stakes leadership, narrative precision is not cosmetic. It is character.

Narrative precision is not cosmetic. It is character.

The words attached to your name — on a website, in a brochure, in a video — aren't "just copy." They are part of your public integrity. And once a story escapes into the wild, you don't get to decide how people repeat it, reinterpret it, or twist it into a joke.

You only get to decide how carefully you told it in the first place.

FIELD NOTES: WHAT THE CAMPAIGNS TAUGHT ME

When I look back on David Knowles' Assembly race — the narrow loss, the unexpected victory two years later, the moments of miscalculation, and the sharp moments of insight — what stands out is not the political mechanics.

It's what those campaigns taught me about how human beings decide what is true.

Because campaigns are leadership under pressure with a clock running. They compress every vulnerability. They expose every assumption. They reveal what matters when you don't have time for explanations and the audience is making judgments with incomplete information.

And that last phrase matters.

In the Knowles races, we learned how frames hold. We learned how frames break. We learned how tiny details — the kind you don't even notice until later — can tilt the whole story. And we learned something that would come back to haunt me more than once: **when you leave blanks in your own narrative, the world will fill them in.**

Here are the takeaways that emerged most clearly.

1. SMALL DETAILS ARE NOT SMALL

Campaigns rarely collapse because of one spectacular failure. More often they collapse because of a dozen small, preventable lapses that never look important until the scoreboard makes them permanent.

The Deukmejian letter didn't fail because the message was wrong. It failed because of a postage shortfall measured in dollars, not thousands. The trays sat on a dock. The final days passed. The voters never saw what could have been the most persuasive piece in the closing stretch.

Most leadership failures arrive like that — quietly, through neglected details that seemed too minor to deserve a meeting.

If you want trust, you don't build it with grand gestures. You build it through discipline around the small things, because small things accumulate.

2. PEOPLE MAKE THE DIFFERENCE THAT MONEY CANNOT

In the rematch, we were outspent five to one. Under normal conditions, that's fatal.

But we had something money couldn't buy: an army of volunteers who believed the work mattered. The California Republican Assembly showed up, built networks, moved through church communities, worked phones, ran precinct efforts — not for recognition, but because they were committed.

Leadership is often described as vision. But vision doesn't carry the load by itself.

People carry the load. And the right people — trusted, committed, value-driven — can compensate for a shocking number of resource gaps.

3. THE FIRST STORY SET IS THE HARDEST TO DISLODGE

Norm Waters' campaign did something smart: they didn't wait for the attacks. They built a frame first.

"The Last Rancher."

A rough-edged, plainspoken local who didn't filter every sentence through politics. In that frame, even a damaging clip — a moment that should have cut sharply — could be dulled into texture. That's just who he is.

The first story people believe becomes the filter they use to interpret everything else. It becomes the lens through which new information is processed.

Which means if you want to change minds, you rarely win by arguing details inside someone else's frame.

You win by changing the frame.

4. AUTHENTICITY MUST BE REAL

The brilliance of "The Last Rancher" frame was not the slogan. It was the emotional coherence. It felt believable.

Until it didn't.

When the parody ad landed, it didn't attack Waters' policies. It attacked the story around him. It made the rancher persona look manufactured — a costume stitched together in a back room.

That's why it worked. Parody punctures with a smile. It doesn't have to prove a case. It only has to make the audience feel the story is off-key.

And once people doubt the authenticity of the frame, the frame stops protecting.

The same is true in every arena of leadership. Audiences don't demand perfection. But they do demand consistency. Authenticity that is real withstands scrutiny. Authenticity that is manufactured collapses on contact.

5. STORY IS THE STRATEGY

We won the rematch with a fraction of the resources because the frame shifted. The "B.S." clip didn't suddenly become more persuasive. The audience simply became more open to receiving it.

That is the central lesson of narrative framing: people don't act based on information. People act based on the stories they believe about that information.

Strategy is narrative. Leadership is narrative. Culture is narrative. Brand is narrative.

And the strongest organizations don't just deliver messages — they shape meaning.

6. BLANK SPACES ARE AN INVITATION

The Knowles campaigns taught me how opponents build frames around you. Later I learned something worse: sometimes they don't have to build anything. They just step into the space you left open.

I saw it in a congressional race that looked flawless on paper. The mail was sharp. The ads tested well. The candidate was charismatic and credible.

But his biography felt unfinished. Not false — just incomplete, like a paragraph had been cut and the seams pressed together.

We rewrote. Polished. Smoothed.

But the gap stayed.

When the attacks hit, they weren't built on proof. They were built on a question:

"What do we really know about this guy?"

"What's he hiding?"

And once that question takes hold, it doesn't need evidence. It only needs a story.

If you don't close the blanks in your own narrative, someone else will.

7. NARRATIVE PRECISION ISN'T COSMETIC, IT'S CHARACTER

Sometimes the blank space isn't omission. It's a detail.

During Dick Mountjoy's U.S. Senate run, we uploaded an old tribute video to the campaign website — an easy way to introduce him quickly.

Buried inside was a line no one had questioned for years: he served in Korea aboard the USS Missouri. It sounded right.

A reporter checked. The ship was wrong. Dick had served honorably — same war, same danger — just on a heavy cruiser, not the Missouri.

In a campaign, that's all it takes.

The opposition didn't have to prove deceit. They only had to attach a frame:

"If he's wrong about his own story, what else is he wrong about?"

We corrected the record. Clarified the facts. Scrubbed the reference.

It didn't matter. The story had already escaped.

That's when I learned the line I've carried ever since: Narrative precision is not cosmetic. It is character.

CLOSING THOUGHT

When I think back to the Knowles race — the 702-vote loss and the 1,500-vote victory — I don't remember the mechanics as much as I remember the feeling of how quickly reality can shift when the story shifts.

Frames decide outcomes long before the final message is delivered. And blank spaces decide outcomes long before you realize you left them.

The better you become at setting the frame — clear, true, compelling — and the more disciplined you become about closing the gaps in your own story, the more influence you will have.

Not just in campaigns.

In any arena where people must choose a direction.

CHAPTER 9

THE MOVEMENT THAT SPLIT ITSELF

Going back to my role with Jack Kemp's presidential campaign, it all began with a letter I wrote to a man named Clark Durant.

It was 1985. Reagan was still in his second term, but the political world was already turning its eyes to 1988. And I knew where mine were pointed: Jack Kemp. His speech at the Republican National Convention had grabbed something inside me, something that hadn't existed when I first stepped onto the University of Michigan campus.

Reagan inspired me. Kemp moved me.

He talked like America was a coiled spring waiting for someone brave enough to release it. He didn't just explain the country — he championed it. And I wanted to be part of the team behind him.

Michigan had just changed its process for 1988, moving the date of its caucuses to January. Overnight, Michigan became the first true battleground. If a candidate could organize precinct delegates here, he could walk into the rest of the country with momentum no poll could capture.

And sitting in Detroit was the man coordinating the whole effort: Clark Durant. He was a Detroit attorney with deep conservative roots, tapped by President Reagan to serve on, and later chair, the board of the Legal Services Corporation. In Michigan, he now headed the Michigan Opportunity Society (MOS), the political committee created to turn Jack Kemp's ideas into a real delegate operation on the ground.

So I wrote him.

It wasn't a long letter, more enthusiasm than eloquence, but I told him I wanted to help — to put my energy behind someone who could actually continue the Reagan revolution.

A few days later, the phone rang:

"We're stuffing envelopes this Saturday," the voice said. "Can you be here?"

There was only one problem.

It was Michigan vs. Notre Dame at the Big House.

Missing a home game? That's a crime.

But enthusiasm can override tradition, and this was the first time anyone from a real presidential effort had asked me to show up. So I sold my game ticket, put on my best Michigan sweatshirt, and drove to Detroit.

When I walked into the Michigan Opportunity Society that Saturday morning, it wasn't a campaign bunker or a cluttered volunteer room. MOS operated out of Clark's law firm, housed on the top floor of the Penobscot Building — one of Detroit's most iconic skyscrapers. The elevator doors opened into a polished reception area lined with dark wood and framed legal credentials, the kind of place where clients expected perfection, not the coming frenzy of a presidential effort.

The views were amazing — windows framed the Detroit River, with Canada stretching out in quiet blue on the other side.

The guy running the room that day was Andy Anuzis, MOS's political director. A few years earlier, he'd been a UM-Dearborn senior starting a scrappy little journal called *Advise and Dissent* so kids could argue Hobbes and Hayek over bologna sandwiches. By 1985, he was widely regarded as one of the most promising young strategists in Michigan. Poised, articulate, and unusually sophisticated for his age, Andy had a calm, collected charm that drew people to him, and an instinctive feel for power and persuasion that made seasoned operatives pay attention.

He greeted me with a nod and a seasoned ease, and immediately put me to work.

A little while later, Clark bounded in wearing a Notre Dame sweater. We all shared a laugh. It was an instant connection — the kind that says: *we may be competitors on the field, but today, we're fighting for the same future.*

That day hooked me. I kept returning. I kept volunteering.

And MOS became more than a committee. It became a community — full of contradictions, energy, tension, humor, and purpose. African-American pastors from Detroit, long-time establishment Republicans talking with young activists who had never attended a county convention in their lives, and volunteers who wore suits sitting beside those who wore jeans and sweatshirts.

That was Kemp's appeal. He crossed boundaries most politicians didn't even acknowledge.

He was conservative, yes, but he was also wildly optimistic and relentlessly inclusive. He could walk into a black church in Detroit and be welcomed as warmly as he was at a country club in Bloomfield Hills. His coalition wasn't theoretical; it was visible in every MOS meeting.

After I graduated, Clark and Andy didn't just thank me — they hired me.

I didn't feel ready — not truly — but the strange thing about campaigns is that readiness is a luxury. Momentum doesn't wait. Delegates don't appear on their own. Coalitions don't build themselves. And politics respects preparation, but moves even when people aren't prepared.

It was the beginning of a journey that would teach me how movements grow, how they fracture, how narratives rise and collapse — and how leadership can be undone not by opposition, but by divergence inside your own ranks.

And it all began because I sold a football ticket, showed up, and stuffed envelopes in a Detroit office filled with people who believed stories could shape the future.

That belief would carry me into the best and worst moments of the Kemp campaign. It would carry me to Mackinac Island. And it would carry me into a confrontation that nearly derailed my standing inside the movement altogether.

BUILDING THE MACHINE

The office had spilled into an entire wing of the law firm, buzzing with the kind of intensity that only comes when a deadline is sprinting toward you. And we had a very real deadline: precinct delegate elections were rapidly approaching.

My role was organizational. Computers. Data. Logistics. I built the tracking systems for every precinct delegate candidate we supported. I helped the field coordinators in every corner of the state. I worked the nuts and bolts and the pieces that had to function smoothly long before strategy could make sense.

As MOS grew, outside consultants were brought in to help with the strategic side of the race. And the immediate mission was clear: prepare thousands of customized mailers for every delegate we were supporting and get them out the door. Our volunteer center became a mail-processing factory. We drove cards

71

around the state so delegates could use them in their own campaigning. For weeks, everything revolved around one outcome: elect as many loyal precinct delegates as possible.

When election day came, the question was simple: How many did we win? The answer changed everything.

Once we saw the numbers, it was obvious: Jack Kemp could not outright win Michigan in a straight head-to-head. We needed a different approach. The campaign shifted overnight from a traditional win-the-state operation to one of influence, coalition building, and convention strategy. And that shift marked the end of MOS as it had existed.

The official Jack Kemp for President campaign took over. New leadership arrived. Old rhythms disappeared. Everything became sharper, faster, more layered.

I was the only MOS staffer brought into the new structure — a transition that felt both sudden and inevitable. The foundational builders, Clark Durant and Andy Anuzis, remained important, but their roles changed. They became the respected public faces of the operation while the national campaign brought in professional strategists to scale the effort.

Two new additions shaped the months ahead, each in a different way.

Paul Welday was a familiar presence in Oakland County GOP politics, valuable not just for strategy but for connection. He knew everyone — donors, precinct captains, county chairs, business leaders, suburban volunteers, and the union workers who quietly decide elections. Paul's gift wasn't writing the playbook; it was knowing who needed to be on the field. He could open doors with a single phone call.

Dick Minard, on the other hand, was the strategist and stabilizer. With decades of political experience behind him, he brought the calm competence that campaigns depend on when the pressure spikes. Dick understood the full terrain — precinct delegates, county conventions, coalition math, and the fragile internal dynamics of a divided Michigan GOP. In caucus politics, where rules and procedure can shift an entire race, his steadiness gave the operation its center.

Paul opened doors. Dick knew what to do once you walked through them.

Together, they gave the campaign exactly what it needed: relationships on one side, strategic discipline on the other — a balance the field team, myself included, would rely on as we pushed those connections into votes, delegates, and momentum on the ground.

THE ANATOMY OF A CAUCUS FIGHT

Primaries are simple: find voters, get them to the polls, hope turnout breaks your way.

Caucuses are something else entirely. To win a caucus state, a campaign must:

1. Recruit precinct delegate candidates.
2. Help them win their precinct elections.
3. Bring them to county conventions to elect county delegates.
4. Bring those delegates to the state convention where the presidential preferences are decided.

It's slow. It's layered. And it's profoundly personal.

Delegate campaigns live or die not by television ads but by small gatherings — living rooms, church basements, union halls, community centers — where twenty people can determine whether your candidate gets one delegate or a dozen.

This is where Pat Robertson's strength became impossible to ignore.

Robertson had entered the race like a lightning strike. He wasn't a traditional political figure. He was a television personality, a preacher, a man whose followers were fueled by a conviction deeper than policy. Church members who had never voted in a primary suddenly found themselves at county meetings and precinct caucuses. The influx was dramatic — and destabilizing.

He had energy. He had new voters. He had structure. And he had a strategy. Suddenly, the once-stable caucus landscape felt like shifting sand.

Our job — *my* job — was to hold Kemp's coalition together and build a delegate slate strong enough to withstand both Robertson's surge and the Bush machine. It meant long nights, endless phone calls, county conventions stretching past midnight, and delicate conversations with people who agreed with us ideologically but were being pulled in multiple directions.

And beneath all of it ran the quiet truth we couldn't ignore:

We had internal fractures of our own.

A CAMPAIGN OF CONTRASTS

On one hand, the Kemp coalition was broad and passionate. You could attend a breakfast in Detroit where inner-city pastors spoke about economic empowerment, and by lunchtime, be in a suburban restaurant with long-established Republican volunteers who had been voting since Eisenhower. Kemp's message — growth, opportunity, expansion — had a reach few conservative candidates could match.

On the other hand, the campaign machinery didn't always reflect that breadth. The resources didn't match the enthusiasm. The execution didn't match the vision.

I still remember the photocopies.

In an era before digital design, photocopied newsletters were the currency of campaign communication. Bob Dole's team sent polished weekly updates on crisp white paper with clean layouts and sharp photos. Ours were often third- or fourth-generation copies, grainy images barely recognizable, text fading like a ghost of what it was meant to be.

It didn't sit well with me.

We were trying to compete in a major national campaign with materials that looked like they'd been rescued from the bottom of someone's filing cabinet.

I finally confronted Dick Minard about it. I expected a sympathetic ear, maybe even a promise that we'd improve.

Instead, he snapped.

He talked about the "echo chamber" — how complaints echo back, how negativity sticks, how reputations calcify. His message was blunt: in politics, you pick your moments and your battles, and complaining about the cosmetics of a campaign could brand me as a problem rather than a solution.

I didn't agree with him. I still don't. Quality mattered. Perception mattered. Narrative mattered.

But I understood what he was trying to teach me: Discretion is part of discipline.

You must know when to speak — and when to hold the line.

At the time, I handled that lesson gracefully. But in the months ahead, I would learn just how thin the line can be between productive friction and destructive fracture.

Because the real test wasn't photocopies. It was the coalition itself.

The movement that had carried us through the early stages of the campaign — diverse, unified, passionate — was about to be pulled apart from the inside.

One question, from one man, at one reception on Mackinac Island would turn the cracks into a chasm. And I was standing right in the middle of it.

MACKINAC ISLAND

The old guard of the Republican Party didn't know what to do with Robertson and his supporters. Some welcomed the enthusiasm. Others panicked. Many simply felt threatened.

And the tension wasn't theoretical. It showed up in every conversation, every meeting, every whispered speculation about whether the GOP was being taken over by religious zealots or being strengthened by a moral backbone long missing.

Inside the Kemp coalition, the shift was even more pronounced. Many early Kemp supporters came from evangelical backgrounds. Some switched their allegiance to Robertson. Others stuck with Kemp.

Suddenly, it wasn't a two-person race between Kemp and Bush. It was a triangulated struggle for the soul of the conservative movement.

And all of that tension followed us to Mackinac Island.

It was an evening reception — the kind where the lighting is soft, the drinks are strong, and the conversations switch from polite to pointed once people settle into the atmosphere. I was mingling with a couple of friends, not expecting anything dramatic. At that stage, I still believed in the illusion that politics could have "calm nights."

Then Neil Bush stepped beside me.

He was charming, approachable, and far more relaxed than anyone might expect from the son of the sitting Vice President. We'd exchanged pleasantries earlier in the weekend. Nothing confrontational. Nothing memorable.

But this time, he cut straight to it.

"So," he said, glancing toward the crowd, "what do you think about all these people Robertson is bringing into the party?"

It wasn't the words. It was the tone.

It carried the unmistakable air of someone who didn't approve of the newcomers — who saw them not as allies, but as intruders. It was a question born of establishment anxiety, the worry that the party might be slipping out of the hands of those who had always controlled it.

It rubbed me the wrong way instantly.

Maybe it was youth. Maybe ego. Maybe the feeling of being caught between two movements I respected — one rooted in policy and optimism, the other in moral conviction and spiritual energy.

Whatever the reason, I reacted poorly.

I pushed back harder than I should have. Much harder.

The conversation spiraled into a sharp exchange — one that crossed lines I shouldn't have crossed, including a cheap shot questioning George Bush's pro-life credentials based on comments made by Barbara Bush.

It was a moment where pride overshadowed prudence.

I don't remember the exact words, but I remember the heat of it — the sense that I had stepped beyond debate into territory where nothing productive could grow.

About that time, Walt White — a friend from UM who was working for the Bush campaign — grabbed me by the arm, pulled me outside, and delivered a riot act worthy of boot camp.

He wasn't wrong. He was furious because he expected more from me — and because he understood something I didn't yet: politics remembers. Not everything, not always accurately, but enough to shape reputations in ways that linger far beyond a single night.

For the rest of the weekend, I was radioactive. I wasn't banned, but it felt close. The Bush supporters avoided me in that polite but unmistakable political way — the sideways glance, the half-nod, the sudden need to be somewhere else.

It was miserable. It was deserved.

THE APOLOGY

On the final morning, bags packed and ferries waiting, I caught sight of Neil Bush. I walked toward him — no entourage or crowd noise to soften the awkwardness.

"I was out of line," I told him.

He nodded. "I appreciate that," he said.

And that was that. We shook hands. No hard feelings.

We ran into each other again in Iowa months later, and by then the incident was a footnote — a moment two young men had moved past.

But the lesson stuck with me:

Leadership begins with controlling the story you tell about yourself — even when emotions are high.

In that moment on Mackinac, I had handed control of my story to impulse.

It wouldn't be the last time I saw narrative slip through my fingers during the Kemp campaign. But it was the first time I recognized how quickly a movement can fracture on the inside.

And the fracture was coming.

Not because of Robertson or Bush. But because our own coalition — the one we had worked so hard to build — no longer agreed on the story we were living.

The break would come soon, and it would be loud.

THE FRACTURE

For all the chaos at Mackinac, it was only a preview. The real break inside the Kemp movement came later, when pressure stopped being theoretical and became unavoidable.

By late 1987, the caucus rhythm was relentless — long days, late nights, endless drives between county meetings. I spent most of my time in Southeast Michigan, building delegate slates one county at a time and trying to keep the coalition steady. On paper, we were still unified. In practice, two competing stories were forming beneath the surface.

One story was driven by hard math: Kemp couldn't win Michigan outright. Pat Robertson's entry had split the conservative base, and against the machinery of a sitting Vice President, that division was fatal. The only viable strategy was to work with Robertson's campaign to block a Bush victory — even if that meant Robertson winning Michigan with Kemp in second place.

The other story belonged to those who feared Robertson's rise. His campaign had activated an entirely new set of evangelical Christians — highly motivated, deeply committed, and new to the Republican Party. They filled precinct delegate slots with near-military discipline. To some in the old guard, this felt less like reinforcements and more like a takeover. The Bush campaign capitalized on that anxiety, warning that a Robertson victory in Michigan could make him unstoppable. Whether the threat was real or tactical didn't matter.

Fear spreads faster than logic.

Inside our ranks, that fear took root — and the split began.

No two people felt the tension more acutely than Andy and Saul Anuzis. They had been among Kemp's earliest and most loyal supporters. Saul, sharp and politically seasoned, was a respected strategist who would later chair the Michigan Republican Party and even seek the chairmanship of the Republican National Committee. Andy, as MOS's political director, had helped build the movement from the ground up — and would go on to serve in GOP leadership himself as chairman of the 17th District Republican Party. Together, they had poured years of work into Kemp's rise in Michigan.

But as the caucus fight intensified, both began arguing for an alliance with the Bush campaign to stop Robertson. Their reasoning wasn't disloyalty; it was concern — concern about Robertson's national strength, yes, but more specifically about what the delegate and convention battles would mean for the long-term leadership of the Michigan GOP. They feared that many of Robertson's new supporters, while deeply motivated, lacked the experience needed to guide the party through future election cycles.

Others of us, myself included, saw the landscape differently. Robertson had passion, but not national breadth. He might win Michigan or even Iowa, but states like New Hampshire and South Carolina were never going to fall his way. Bush already had the money and the machinery; giving him Michigan would only fuel his inevitability narrative. *If Kemp had any chance at the nomination, Bush needed to be slowed, not strengthened.*

But fear rarely yields to persuasion.

The more we talked, the more the room divided. What began as strategy sessions turned into interventions. Friends who had built the movement together began drifting to opposite sides of the argument. The tension was no longer about policy or ideology — it was about which story each of us believed would save the movement.

And that, more than anything outside our walls, is what fractured us.

THE MEMO

The split became official: a large chunk of the Kemp team was now working with Bush. Confusion spread quickly, and rumors traveled even faster. Delegates wanted to know who spoke for whom. Lines were blurring, and the sense of a unified Kemp effort was evaporating.

At some point, the pressure became too much. I sat down and wrote a memo.

It was direct and emotional, born out of urgency. Delegates needed clarity, and I needed to protect the movement we had been building. My goal was straightforward: to make sure our delegates understood that Andy's position did not represent the official Kemp campaign. The coalition was fracturing, and I felt responsible for holding the center together before the rift became permanent.

But in that attempt, I went too far. I didn't just correct the record; I disavowed Andy — my friend, mentor, and one of the first people to bring me into the campaign. At the time, it felt like the necessary stand. Looking back, it wasn't the message itself that was wrong, but the way I delivered it. Passion outran judgment. I can write a sharp memo when pushed. This one cut deeper than it needed to.

THE COUNTY CONVENTIONS

When the county conventions arrived, the divide was fully exposed. Delegates loyal to Kemp and Robertson walked into meetings believing they had the numbers to control the process. The Bush delegates, aligned with parts of our own coalition, believed the same.

Arguments erupted over rules and credentials. One county convention devolved into something close to procedural warfare. You could feel decades of party tradition cracking under the weight of three factions pulling in different directions.

This wasn't a policy fight. It wasn't ideological. It was a narrative crisis.

No one agreed on who we were anymore. No one agreed on the story.

THE STATE CONVENTION — AND THE WALKOUT

The state convention that followed was the most chaotic political event I have ever experienced. The divide that began as a hairline fracture had become a canyon.

The official Kemp team joined the alignment with the Bush coalition to maintain influence over the delegates. Many of my closest friends, however, had joined the Robertson-Kemp alliance downstairs, forming what became known as a rump convention. Their argument was simple: the official process was illegitimate, and they held the true majority.

I stood between them — literally and emotionally.

Downstairs, the Robertson-Kemp crowd filled the room with energy and defiance. The moment took an unexpected turn when Pat Robertson himself made a surprise appearance. The place erupted. For them, this was a revolution of the grassroots reclaiming the party.

Upstairs, the official convention plowed forward. Delegates were counted, rules enforced, and alliances solidified.

Two competing stories played out simultaneously on different floors of the same building. Only one would end up recorded in the official results.

And the official story was clear: George H. W. Bush won Michigan.

That was the headline.

But the emotional cost was greater than the political one. The coalition that had once united suburban Republicans, young activists, inner-city pastors, and evangelical Christians had fractured so completely that it would never be fully rebuilt.

THE AFTERMATH

When I look back now, the pain doesn't come from the loss. Politics is full of losses. You learn to absorb them.

The pain comes from knowing that we didn't lose to Bush or Robertson. We lost to ourselves.

We weren't defeated by a better message.

We weren't outworked.

We weren't outmaneuvered.

We simply stopped telling the same story.

We weren't defeated by a better message. We simply stopped telling the same story.

And once the story splintered, the movement followed.

Movements don't collapse because of attacks from the outside. They collapse when they stop agreeing on the story that defines who they are.

Movements don't collapse because of attacks from the outside. They collapse when they stop agreeing on the story that defines who they are.

And the cost — whether measured in votes, friendships, or momentum — is always higher than anyone imagines in the beginning.

FINAL BEAT

When the dust settled after the Michigan state convention, the most striking feeling wasn't anger or disappointment. It was emptiness — the kind that follows a story that didn't just end, but collapsed under its own weight. The Kemp movement in Michigan hadn't been defeated in a dramatic showdown. It had simply come apart, piece by piece, as if the inner stitching had unraveled faster than anyone could repair it.

The fracture revealed something I had never fully understood, even though I had lived through the signs.

A movement isn't held together by organizational charts. It isn't sustained by press releases or endorsements. It doesn't rise or fall on who shows up to a county meeting.

A movement survives — or dies — on the strength of the story its people believe.

In Michigan, we stopped believing the same story.

Some believed we were on the brink of resetting the national race.

Some believed we needed to stop Pat Robertson at all costs.

Some believed we were defending the soul of conservatism.

Some believed we were clinging to something already slipping away.

All of those stories had their own logic. None of them could coexist.

THE FIGHT OVER MEANING

There is a moment in every leader's journey when you realize the battle you think you're fighting is rarely the battle you're actually in. Policy fights, budget fights, campaign fights — these look like contests of message, discipline, or resources. But beneath all that machinery lies the real contest: the fight over meaning. The story people use to interpret what they're seeing.

Looking back on the stories in this section — the State Assembly race, the congressional campaign with the incomplete biography, the Mountjoy Senate race, and the splintering inside the Kemp coalition in Michigan — I see the same lesson emerging again and again: **People do not respond to facts until those facts fit a frame.** And if a leader does not supply that frame, someone else will.

In California, the "Last Rancher" frame nearly protected an incumbent — until a parody revealed the gap between the story and the truth. The congressional candidate's campaign collapsed not from opposition research but from gaps we left in his own story. Dick Mountjoy's integrity was unquestioned until one sentence in a video rewrote his narrative overnight. In Michigan, the Kemp movement didn't fall apart because of ideology; it fell apart because people stopped agreeing on the story that held them together.

Across all of it, the pattern is unmistakable: Frames pull people together or push them apart. Frames clarify identity or muddle it. Frames create unity or create drift.

The most important insight is not how quickly narratives can shift. It's how quietly they do.

Groups rarely fracture because of conflict alone. They fracture because of competing interpretations — private meanings that grow in the absence of shared meaning. Two people can experience the same moment and walk away convinced they lived through two completely different realities.

That realization becomes personal for every leader. I saw it in Michigan when the coalition around Kemp split into competing stories. I saw it again later in creative work, where unspoken expectations created a narrative gap that eventually collapsed a project.

Narrative integrity is not about better spin. It's about deeper truth.

If Part I taught clarity, and Part II taught precision, then Part III teaches something even more foundational:

Leadership requires the discipline to frame reality in a way that is honest, coherent, and shared.

When leaders fail to frame the moment, people supply meanings of their own — and those meanings rarely align with the mission. Teams drift. Coalitions strain. Movements lose their center. But when leaders name the moment, reveal the stakes, and give people a shared interpretation, even difficult seasons become unifying ones.

Leadership in this section isn't about messaging. It's about translation.

It's the ability to take complexity, tension, ego, hope, and uncertainty and shape them into a story people can stand inside together.

OWN THE FRAME

There is a moment in every organization when people stop debating facts and start negotiating meaning. They aren't asking what happened. They're asking what this means for us.

Don't start with messaging. Start with meaning.

Narrative isn't spin. It's the frame people use to interpret reality. And if you don't supply that frame, someone else will — quietly, quickly, and rarely in your favor.

If you want narrative to work for you instead of against you, begin here.

1. NAME THE FRAME BEFORE SILENCE FILLS IT

A frame will form whether you speak or not. Silence doesn't preserve neutrality — it invites interpretation.

When leaders delay meaning, people supply their own:

- Rumors become explanations
- Assumptions become beliefs
- Frustration becomes story

Name the moment early. Define what this season is and what it is not.

The first story people hear becomes the filter through which they judge everything that follows.

If you wait, you don't stay neutral. You surrender control.

2. MAKE SURE EVERYONE KNOWS WHICH STORY THEY'RE IN

Most breakdowns don't come from disagreement. They come from people living in different stories at the same time.

Some think they're rebuilding. Some think they're defending. Some think they're surviving. Some think they're transforming.

Clarify the shared narrative:

- "This is a stabilization season, not an expansion one."

- "Right now, we are protecting trust, not chasing growth."
- "This moment is about coherence, not speed."

People can tolerate difficulty. They can't tolerate ambiguity about why it exists.

3. ALIGN THE FRAME WITH WHO YOU ACTUALLY ARE

Frames only hold when they match reality. Jack Kemp at a UPS facility at dawn worked because it was true. "The Last Rancher" worked only until parody revealed it wasn't.

If the frame doesn't fit your identity:
- Even success feels hollow
- Even victories weaken trust
- Even applause sounds thin

Narrative isn't aspiration. It's coherence. People forgive limits. They don't forgive falseness. The camera always knows. So does your team.

4. SURFACE COMPETING NARRATIVES BEFORE THEY HARDEN

Unspoken stories don't dissolve. They ferment.

If you sense drift, name it:
- "I'm hearing two interpretations. We need one."
- "Some believe this means X. Others believe Y."
- "Let's be clear about the story we're telling ourselves."

The Kemp coalition didn't fracture in public. It fractured in private conversations left unaddressed.

Silence doesn't keep peace. It creates factions.

5. PROTECT THE FRAME WITH INTEGRITY, NOT SPIN

Narrative power collapses the moment truth bends.

The Mountjoy campaign didn't fall because of intent — it fell because one sentence contradicted the story people trusted.

Protect the frame by protecting reality:
- Don't exaggerate wins
- Don't minimize losses

- Don't leave gaps others can fill
- Don't pretend unity exists when it doesn't

If you leave blanks in your story, the world will fill them in — and never in your favor.

Narrative integrity isn't cosmetic. It's character made public.

A CLOSING DISCIPLINE

If you want one place to begin, begin here: at the end of every major decision, ask one question: What story will people tell themselves about this tomorrow? Then act accordingly.

But this only works if you answer the deeper question in private first. Here is what this requires of you when no one is watching: examine the story you are telling yourself before you speak to anyone else. Notice where fear is writing your frame. Notice where ego is steering the interpretation. Notice where silence is tempting you because you don't want the discomfort of naming reality.

Clarify meaning before messaging. Name reality before opinions calcify. Align the story with truth before momentum outruns integrity.

Movements don't fracture because of pressure. They fracture because the story underneath them no longer makes sense. Your job as a leader is not to control every outcome. It is to steady the meaning of the moment — and that steadiness begins in the unseen discipline of a leader who refuses to let private interpretations drift from public truth.

People don't follow leaders. They follow the story leaders help them make sense of.

THE HUMAN STORY: FAILURE, FAITH & REINVENTION

CHAPTER 10

THE FILM THAT
ALMOST HAPPENED

The first three sections of this book have focused outward — on the clarity you give teams, the precision you model, and the narratives you shape in organizations and movements. These are essential leadership skills. They work. I've used them to run campaigns, build teams, shape messages, and influence outcomes.

But they rest on an assumption that breaks down the moment you face real crisis: they assume the leader is whole.

The truth is, most leadership books skip the chapter where the leader breaks. Where the story you're telling the world diverges from the story you're living. Where the confidence you project begins to crack under the weight of what's actually happening inside you. Where clarity, precision, and narrative control mean nothing because you can't see straight anymore.

I've watched leaders master the external skills — everything I've taught in Parts I through III — only to see them crumble when their internal foundation gave way. I know what that looks like because I've been that leader. The one who knew how to frame a message for others but couldn't face the truth about his own story.

Before you can lead anyone else through their story, you must first be able to navigate your own. Before you can offer clarity to a confused team, you must find it within yourself when everything you've built threatens to collapse. Before you can call others to precision, you must face your own failures. Before you can frame a movement's narrative, you must reframe the story you tell yourself when the ground gives way beneath you.

Part IV isn't about techniques or tactics. It's about survival. It's about what happens when the leader faces failure, when faith is tested, and when reinvention becomes the only path forward.

This is the chapter most leadership books avoid. But it's the one that determines whether everything else you've learned will actually hold when life comes at you full force.

> ## Before you can lead anyone else through their story, you must first be able to navigate your own.

BACK INTO THE ARENA

There are seasons in life when the pace of the world seems to match the pace of your spirit — when doors open with surprising ease, when momentum feels natural rather than forced, when the forward motion seems to have its own internal compass. The years leading into the new century were like that for me.

Between my earlier campaign work and returning to California politics, I had spent five years working internationally with a ministry organization. That chapter — which I'll share fully in Part V — reshaped how I understood leadership, influence, and purpose. I had learned to write under pressure, produce television in challenging conditions, and lead in environments where clarity wasn't optional. More importantly, I had been formed by leaders whose integrity and purpose ran deeper than ambition.

When that season ended, and it was time to return to politics, I came back different. Not just with new skills, but with a reoriented compass. I wanted to see if everything I'd learned in that crucible could survive the noise of California campaigns, the speed of political messaging, and the pressure of winning and losing.

And almost overnight, the doors flung open.

The year was 1998. Within months, I found myself back in the world I had left behind — precinct lists, messaging plans, walk pieces, and television spots. But I wasn't the same person who had left.

I wasn't just a strategist anymore. I could write. I could shoot. I could edit. I could design. I could buy airtime. I could build the narrative, then shape the tools that carried it.

Business boomed. Campaigns flowed toward me like water toward a downhill path. My new skillset — strategy, messaging, design, production, media buying — made me a kind of one-man communications engine, and in politics, the ability to both conceive a message and deliver it visually is a superpower. My business took off. Race after race, cycle after cycle, my name showed up on reports across the state. One year at the Legislative Softball Game, I looked down the roster of Republican members and realized I had touched nearly all their campaigns in one way or another.

It was frenetic and exciting and exhausting and rewarding all at once. And in the middle of all of it, life felt... stable. Good. Predictable. The years that followed were full: clients, victories, late nights, deadlines, strategy sessions that stretched into dawn. I was working at full speed, carrying the confidence of someone who had found his lane.

WHEN EVERYTHING CHANGES

It was October 2004 — the peak of campaign season. My desk was buried under schedules, budgets, mail proofs. Election Day loomed like a storm.

Late one night, Cathy called from upstairs.

"Jeff... something's wrong."

I ran up to find her sitting upright, eyes closed, her body twitching in a way I had never seen. She insisted she was fine. Just indigestion. She even asked for a Diet Coke and told me to get back to work. I didn't. I lay awake beside her, listening to her breathing until morning.

By daylight, she seemed fine. But after her shower, she said quietly, "I think you should take me to the ER." She insisted I drop her off and return to the office — campaign schedules wait for no one — and against my instincts, I did.

An hour later, the hospital called.

A doctor's voice, urgent but controlled, told me Cathy had suffered a heart attack. They were rushing her into a procedure. The world of politics, deadlines, and clients disappeared in an instant.

She made it through the first stent, and for a moment, we let ourselves breathe. But days later, she said her heart felt "strange." Back to the ER. A different cardiologist this time, studying scans with a frown.

"Why didn't they treat the other blockage?"

Her second artery had been compromised too. Doctors would later say they weren't sure how she survived the first event. Procedures followed. More nights in sterile rooms. More phrases no spouse wants to hear.

And then, on my birthday, surgeons performed a five-way bypass.

Three grafts collapsed within weeks. More surgeries, more stents, more conversations with physicians trying to stay calm while delivering truths no one wants to speak.

Finally, the prognosis: "We don't know if she'll make it five years."

Five years.

We had a twelve-year-old son at home. A daughter just beginning her life in Ohio. And a future suddenly reduced to a number.

STORYTELLING CALLS ME BACK

We changed everything — diet, lifestyle, priorities. We took the kids to Europe. It wasn't a vacation; it was gratitude. A reminder that time is borrowed.

And in the space between fear and hope, something long buried resurfaced. Before politics, before campaigns swallowed my life, I had loved storytelling — first onstage, later through television. My dream had been *NBC Nightly News*. Life pulled me elsewhere, and I let it.

After Cathy's heart attack, ambition lost some of its noise. And storytelling — real storytelling — called me back.

I saw an ad for Dov S.S. Simens' three-day film school in San Francisco. A weekend crash course in filmmaking. I signed up immediately. It felt reckless. It felt necessary.

Simens was electric — blunt, inspiring, unwavering. I left convinced I could write a screenplay. So I did.

Power & Pride poured out of me. For weeks, I lived inside the script.

THE COLLAPSE

After polishing many drafts, I reached out to the most Hollywood-connected person I knew: Ted Baehr of *MovieGuide*. He gave me the advice that could have saved me: "Work within the system. Let Hollywood do it."

But I had imagined something different — my script, my story, my son in one of the roles. I convinced myself Hollywood would ruin it. I believed my momentum was divine confirmation. And so I ignored his counsel and chose to produce the film myself.

And incredibly, at first, it worked.

Within three months, half the budget was raised. A production partner committed to the rest. Casting director Toni Suttie landed Stephen Baldwin and Eric Roberts. Before too long, Helen Slater also joined the cast. We booked hotels, hired crew, and signed contracts. The film felt real.

But our main investor kept delaying. Banking issues, international transfers, assurances that the money was "in motion." Momentum is a powerful anesthetic — and I wanted to believe him.

One afternoon, driving my Mercedes convertible on a warm California day, I said aloud, "God, I love my life."

It felt like the beginning of something extraordinary.

It was the calm before the collapse — as the Bible warns, "pride goes before destruction" (Proverbs 16:18).

A week before shooting, Stephen Baldwin called to confirm dates. I told him I'd know more in 24 hours. Then I phoned our partner — and the truth surfaced. The money wasn't coming. Not now. Maybe not ever.

We were sunk.

Production halted. Penalties hit immediately — tens of thousands in hotel guarantees gone, "pay or play" contracts for actors still due, deposits evaporating. I wrote check after check while scrambling to replace the funds.

The 2008 financial crisis was still tearing through the economy. People were losing homes. No one was funding independent films.

I put the production on indefinite hold.

The dream collapsed. Investors — many of them friends — lost money. I lost much of my savings. Months of preparation disappeared. My confidence evaporated. I had stepped out convinced I was following God, following purpose, following momentum — and instead found myself staring at the wreckage of a dream that never made it off the ground.

And I didn't know it then, but this was only the beginning.

LEADERSHIP PRINCIPLE — WHEN MOMENTUM BLINDS YOU

Looking back, the most dangerous part of that season wasn't the film itself. It was the way momentum disguised itself as calling. Early success, open doors, and rapid progress can feel like divine confirmation, but momentum is a terrible substitute for discernment.

Momentum is a terrible substitute for discernment.

I mistook opportunity for permission. I let ego speak with the authority of conviction. And I ignored wise counsel because the story in my head sounded too good to question.

Leaders step into trouble when they let momentum interpret reality for them. Open doors are not the same as green lights. Early wins are not proof of wisdom. And a dream that moves too quickly can blind you to the foundations that were never built.

The next chapter would test me in ways deeper and darker than anything the film had taken away.

The floor was about to give way.

CHAPTER 11

WHEN THE FLOOR GIVES WAY

The year after the film collapsed, life settled into an uneasy rhythm. It was 2010 — another election year — and campaigns have a way of pulling you back into motion, whether you feel ready or not. I threw myself into the work because work was what I knew. Mail to design. Polling to analyze. Television spots to plan. I was still trying to raise new money for the movie in the margins between campaign deadlines, clinging to the hope that the project might still find its footing.

Then one afternoon, I found myself talking with Karl Heft, a friend whose path I had crossed countless times in politics. We were standing in a hallway between convention sessions, the kind of place where conversations usually rush past each other without depth. But that day, I voiced what had been weighing on me: the frustration, the stalled momentum, the sense that I was pushing a boulder up a hill that never leveled out.

Karl listened quietly, his head tilted slightly the way he always did when he was measuring the weight of someone's words. And then he asked the question that stopped me cold.

"Jeff… do you know what I do for a living?"

I laughed, because of course I did — or at least I thought I did. Then he smiled, almost amused by the irony of the moment.

"I raise money for movies."

It felt like someone cracked open a window in a suffocating room. A new start. A second chance I hadn't dared hope for. Within weeks, Karl and I were on conference calls with producers, distributors, investors — people I would never have reached on my own. Every time something unexpected aligned, Karl would shake his head and say, "Jeff, this never happens." And for a brief stretch of time, it felt like the impossible might actually come together.

But the economy still carried the bruises of 2008. Investors who had the will didn't have the capacity. Investors who had the capacity were afraid to take risks. Meetings went well. Doors opened. Promises were made. But nothing landed. Nothing held. Hope became a kind of mirage — shimmering, beautiful, but just out of reach.

Then came 2011.

I had survived the first wave of the economic collapse in 2009 and 2010 by sheer force of will. My political clients were steady; the campaigns kept me afloat. But by 2011, the non-political side of my business — the year-round foundation that sustained us between elections — buckled. One client disappeared, then another. The phone stopped ringing. Projects evaporated.

Our finances followed suit.

We still hadn't recovered the money I had poured into keeping the film alive. The losses sat like stones at the bottom of our accounts. Bills stacked. Income vanished. I watched our savings drain away until there was nothing left to drain. There were months when the simple math of survival didn't add up, and nights when Cathy and I stared at each other without answers.

We came closer to losing our home than I've ever admitted publicly.

I remember standing in the kitchen one night, hands spread on the counter, trying to steady myself against the panic rising in my chest. I had always been the steady one. The one who could figure it out. Now I was a man staring at the edge, trying to hold his family together with nothing but prayer and grit.

And that is where humility finds you — not gently, but in the places where you have no choice but to kneel.

Somehow, by God's grace, we made it through.

The house was saved.

But the ego was gone.

The Mercedes and the Lexus — symbols of a success I once wore too comfortably — were replaced by a single Kia that kept us moving and little else. We had no savings. The bills felt relentless. But we were breathing again. We were still standing. And we were together.

By 2012 — another election year — work began to return. Not the flood I once knew, but enough to catch our balance. Enough to feel purpose again. We rebuilt slowly, month by month, stepping carefully now, more aware than ever of how fragile "success" can be.

The dream of the film never fully left me, but its story changed shape. It became something humbler, something wiser. The loss still stung, but the regret softened. And eventually, I could see the blessing hidden in the collapse.

If the movie had succeeded, it could have launched my son into the heart of Hollywood — a world he wasn't ready for, a world filled with temptations and pressures that might have swallowed him whole. At that time in his life, he didn't have the grounding, the spiritual maturity, the internal ballast to survive that environment.

I had wanted to give him a gift. But looking back, I realized the collapse might have spared him.

What felt like devastation at the time became, in hindsight, protection.

And that is the strange mercy of life: sometimes the floor gives way not to break you, but to keep you from stepping into a room you were never meant to enter.

LEADERSHIP PRINCIPLE — WHEN REALITY CANNOT SUSTAIN THE STORY

The collapse taught me something I had been too proud — and too busy — to see: **the floor never gives way at random.** It gives way at the places where truth and perception no longer match.

In my own life, I had been carrying a story that looked steady from the outside — success, competence, momentum — but inside, the foundation had been thinning for years. I had mistaken motion for strength, progress for stability, confidence for calling. And when pressure finally came, the story I had built around myself could no longer hold the weight of the life I was living.

Collapse is rarely the beginning of failure. It's the revelation of it.

Collapse is rarely the beginning of failure. It's the revelation of it.

What breaks us is not the crisis, but the quiet distance we allowed to grow between who we were and who we pretended to be. And the mercy of collapse is this: it exposes what was never sustainable, giving us the chance to rebuild on something real.

Only then can a leader begin to live a story that doesn't require constant reinforcement, performance, or spin — a story that can withstand pressure because it's built on truth, not perception.

CHAPTER 12

THE STORY YOU TELL YOURSELF

There are certain truths a person only learns when the lights go out.

In politics, I had spent years constructing narratives that moved crowds and motivated coalitions. I knew how to frame a message, how to position a candidate, how to read a room. I understood influence as an architecture you could build if you had the tools and the talent.

None of that prepared me for the moment when the story I told the world no longer matched the story I was living at home.

At first, the difference was small enough to ignore. A missed indicator here, a quiet uneasiness there. I told myself it was nothing — a busy season, a temporary strain, the natural cost of ambition. But over time that gap widened, and the momentum I had once trusted began to feel like a current pulling me somewhere I hadn't intended to go. Momentum is funny that way; it gives the illusion of progress even while the foundation underneath you thins.

In political campaigns, I'd learned how to project confidence, how to amplify a message, how to maintain the appearance of a thriving movement even when it took constant work behind the scenes just to keep the gears from locking.

That worked in politics. But life is not a campaign, and eventually the truth outruns the polish.

When my business faltered, when the film collapsed, when the savings evaporated and the family cars went from luxury to necessity, the distance between my public confidence and my private fear became something I could no longer bridge by sheer will. I had always prided myself on carrying weight others couldn't see, quietly steering through storms by determination alone. But the harder I pushed, the more obvious it became that I wasn't holding anything together anymore. Something was holding *me* — and that something was beginning to give way.

What finally broke wasn't my business. It was my pride.

For years, I had believed I could outwork hardship. The next project would fix things. The next election would reset the balance. The next opportunity would refill what had drained away. I had built my life on a belief that competence, timing, and grit could carry me through anything.

But strength without truth becomes a burden. And a burden carried alone becomes a breaking point.

The day I admitted that I couldn't force my life back into shape was not dramatic. It was quieter than that — almost gentle, like a structure finally settling after years of stress. It was the moment I saw clearly what I had been avoiding: the story I lived and the story I presented were no longer the same story.

That realization brought an ache, but it also brought something else: a turning.

Because if a leader's clarity comes from the story they tell, that story has to start with the one they tell themselves. And my story — my real one — was not about my resilience or my strategic instincts. It was a story about how deeply I still trusted my own strength, even after life had shown me its limits.

The collapse forced me to confront that truth. It brought me to a place where I finally stopped trying to design my way out of trouble and started asking God to lead me out of it. Not as a consultant asking for a talking point, but as a man asking for a lifeline.

Humility didn't feel like virtue at first. It felt like surrender. But that surrender turned out to be the doorway.

When I stopped performing strength and started living honestly again — when I stopped polishing the external narrative and let God reshape the internal one — something steadied in me. Circumstances didn't magically improve. The bills didn't disappear. The wounds didn't instantly heal. But the striving quieted. The frantic grasping eased. My footing returned one inch at a time.

God didn't fix my life overnight. He reshaped *me* instead.

And as that inner work took root, the story I lived slowly realigned with the story I spoke. My identity stopped orbiting success, clients, or campaigns. It settled into something deeper, anchored in the conviction that God had not abandoned me, not even in my missteps, and that the collapse I feared might actually have been a mercy I didn't yet understand.

In time, I learned what all those years of political framing could never teach me: that a leader cannot live two competing stories and remain whole. Not for long.

A leader cannot live two competing stories and remain whole.

When the inner narrative and the outer narrative diverge, the soul splits its strength trying to hold them both. Influence weakens. Confidence thins. Decisions lose clarity. The leader becomes an actor in his own life — performing stability instead of living truth.

But when a leader allows God to bring those two stories together — when identity aligns with honesty, when pride gives way to trust — something shifts. Not loudly. Not suddenly. But undeniably.

There is a freedom in living a true story. A strength in letting an old narrative die. A clarity in surrender that no amount of effort can manufacture.

What I discovered in those years was simple: God was not finished with me. The collapse was not the end of the story. It was the beginning of a truer one.

And that truer story would become the foundation upon which the rest of my life — and my leadership — would be rebuilt. **The story you tell yourself becomes the foundation for everything that follows.** But that story only holds if you live it.

I learned this not through theory, but through watching leaders whose lives matched their words so completely that their presence carried weight without effort. Some of them led quietly. Some led through crisis. But all of them shared one quality: alignment — coherence between who they were and how they led.

When that coherence exists, influence becomes natural. Trust deepens without announcement. Leadership flows from integrity, not performance. These are the stories of people who taught me what that looks like.

UPWARD BASKETBALL

It happened in a beautiful gym in California, where Saturdays echo with the sound of bouncing balls and kids shouting each other's names. Our church hosted an Upward Basketball league — a ministry built on the idea that character matters more than the scoreboard — and when the longtime leaders stepped aside in 2002, I took the reins for two seasons.

That first year, a friend of mine recruited volunteer referees. Most were legislative staffers — men and women who spent their weekdays negotiating policy and pressure, but who showed up on weekends to help kids learn teamwork and grace. They weren't paid. They didn't complain. They simply believed in what we were trying to build.

On the last day of the season, during one of the final games, everything nearly came undone.

A tight contest. The clock winding down. A whistle. A foul.

Free throws were awarded. The opposing team sank the shots. Won the game.

Before I could even register the shift in the room, a father — red-faced, furious, convinced the universe had conspired against his son — sprinted toward the referees, demanding an explanation. His voice echoed across the gym, sharp enough to make a few children freeze.

I stepped forward to intervene, but someone beat me to it.

Jedd Medefind — one of our volunteer refs — turned toward the irate parent with a calm that felt almost out of place in the chaos. He didn't raise his voice or retreat. He simply offered a broad, steady smile and said six quiet words:

"Not in front of the kids."

The whole scene shifted.

The father stopped mid-stride, as if the sentence itself had caught him by the collar. The tension drained just enough for everyone to breathe again. The adults stepped outside, explanations were given, disagreement remained — but the moment that could have become a spectacle never did.

I saw something in Jedd that day — a kind of strength that doesn't announce itself. A servant's heart wrapped in calm authority. A man who understood instinctively that leadership is not measured by who wins an argument, but by who protects the environment where people are learning and growing.

He diffused the moment not through power, but through presence.

And that, more often than not, is where real leadership lives.

WHEN THE MOMENT CALLS YOUR NAME

I still remember the tone of the call — the quiet, clipped urgency only campaign people recognize. We were deep into the 2022 Michigan governor's race, a field crowded with ambition and polished resumes, when the crisis hit. My candidate, Michael Brown, was the kind of man you don't often see in politics anymore: a Marine, a police captain, and a natural leader without ever trying to sound like one. People trusted him instinctively. He didn't talk about integrity; he carried it.

We were building something real. Endorsements were lining up. Donors were leaning in. His story resonated in every room — the kind of lived, earned credibility consultants pray for.

Then came the news.

A signature-gathering vendor we had used — a contractor relied upon by multiple campaigns — was accused by the state of submitting fraudulent signatures. The state invalidated every petition the vendor had handled, affecting multiple campaigns at once — including ours. The deadline was immovable. And the ruling meant Michael Brown, through no fault of his own, would not appear on the ballot.

Inside the campaign, the air shifted.

We scrambled onto a conference call, trying to punch light into the darkness. There were possible legal arguments. Creative appeals. A claim that even if some signatures were bad, the entire sheet shouldn't be rejected. We weighed the options. In politics, there's always a path if you're willing to stretch the map far enough. And this was a moment where stretching the map would have been easy to justify.

We laid every option on the table.

And then Michael spoke.

His voice was steady — almost too calm for the moment. He listened to every argument, asked a couple of clarifying questions, then let out a breath that seemed to carry both weariness and resolve.

"No," he said. "We're not doing this."

There was a pause on the line, the kind that presses into your chest.

He continued.

"I don't want my name connected to anything that even touches wrongdoing — even if it's not ours. Even if we win the appeal, the campaign is overshadowed. Everything we stand for is tainted. Pull the plug."

It was the hardest decision imaginable for a man who had done everything right. And yet, because he made it without hesitation, it became one of the moments I respected him most.

He wasn't protecting his ego or his ambitions. He was protecting his story.

Michael Brown understood something far too many leaders learn too late:

You can recover from losing an election. You cannot easily recover from losing who you are.

The race ended. But his integrity remained intact — clear, unbent, unmistakable.

And long after that campaign faded from the headlines, the memory of that conference call stayed with me. How a true leader carries himself when the spotlight is gone. How character makes decisions that ambition would never choose.

How alignment, not victory, becomes the real legacy.

THE QUIETEST KIND OF INTEGRITY

Not every leader faces their defining moment on a conference call or in the glare of a campaign. Some live it out so quietly you almost miss it.

For many years, I volunteered my services for Sacramento Valley Teen Challenge — designing newsletters, print materials, whatever they needed. It was the local chapter of Teen Challenge International, a ministry born in the grit of addiction recovery and street evangelism. But Sacramento had its own spirit, and that spirit was embodied in one man.

Dick Rhoads.

He was one of the most unassuming leaders I've ever encountered. He had the gentle, almost scholarly air of someone who listened more than he spoke. Nothing rattled him. Nothing inflated him. He oversaw everything — the thrift store, the residential recovery homes, the small army of staff and students rebuilding their lives, and just as important, the fundraising. Teen Challenge survived on donations, not government funding.

And unlike the era's high-profile ministries — the scandals, the excess, the jets — Dick lived in a way that made all of it feel like a different universe. His office was furnished with used furniture. He drove an older sedan. He lived with a quiet, unadvertised simplicity that matched the work he carried.

There was no branding strategy, no personal platform, no curated image. Just alignment. Calling. Consistency.

He wasn't trying to *project* integrity. He was simply living the story he believed.

And in a time when public faith often fractured under spectacle, Dick Rhoads reminded me that some of the strongest leaders are the ones who never raise their voices — the ones whose lives, not their titles, do the teaching.

THE RISE, RAID & REDEMPTION OF PAT NOLAN

Not every test of integrity is loud. Some arrive in the quiet momentum of a career on the rise.

In the late 1980s, Pat Nolan was one of the brightest political stars in California. Sharp, disciplined, and effective, he had risen to become the Assembly Republican Leader, guiding his caucus through a season of real legislative gains. There was talk that he might be governor someday.

Then came the raid.

The FBI launched "Shrimpscam" — an undercover sting where agents posed as shrimp-company executives seeking state help. They offered the legislators legal campaign contributions. Many legislators met with them, accepted the checks, and supported a bill they would have backed anyway on the merits.

Pat was among them.

He met with the "businessmen," accepted their contribution, and later cast a vote he would have cast regardless. The proposal was solid policy, aligned with his principles. But nuance rarely survives a federal investigation. Under immense pressure, a legislative staffer broke and provided damaging testimony — testimony shaped as much by fear as by fact.

The indictment came down. Several lawmakers were charged. Pat was swept into the dragnet.

For months, he shuttled between home and his attorney's office, preparing a defense that, by all accounts, was strong. But the political climate was poisoned. His attorney believed a jury — any jury — would convict a politician at the height of public cynicism, no matter the evidence.

So Pat made the most agonizing decision a father can make: he accepted a plea to a lesser charge so he wouldn't risk losing years of his children's lives. He served his sentence in federal prison — a place no one imagined a man of his character would ever stand.

But something happened there. Something quiet. Something seismic.

Pat later said, "I went to prison believing in God. I came out knowing God."

When the gate finally opened, he didn't walk back into politics. He walked into ministry. He joined Chuck Colson's Prison Fellowship and quickly became a key leader in Justice Fellowship, the reform arm of the organization. Ironically — beautifully — he spent the next phase of his life fighting to reform the very sentencing laws he once supported as a legislator.

Years later, he received a full pardon. But his redemption didn't begin with a document. It began in a cell. And that's what made his story so different from the political redemption arcs I'd witnessed before — this one wasn't scripted; it was surrendered.

Pat Nolan's story is not the story of a politician who fell. It's the story of a man who returned to the core of who he was — not because of success, but because of surrender.

Pat's journey taught me something I've seen repeatedly in leadership: not every fall comes from corruption, and not every rise comes from victory. Sometimes a leader is undone not by intent, but by the climate around them — by assumptions, pressures, and systems that fail to protect truth. And sometimes the truest integrity is forged in the aftermath, when the spotlight is gone, and all that is left is a man and his faith.

Pat walked into prison with a resume. He walked out with a calling.

The man who once championed tough-on-crime laws is spending the rest of his life fighting to heal the system he once trusted. It was costly. It was humbling. And it was real.

Leadership often reveals its truest shape not in the heights we reach, but in the story we choose to live once everything else has been stripped away.

It was a lesson I didn't fully understand then. But I would — the day I met Rosa Parks.

MY ENCOUNTER WITH ROSA PARKS

The National Religious Broadcasters Convention has always had a certain electricity to it — a hum of deals being made in hallways, camera crews weaving through crowds, authors tucked into booths hoping their newest release finds the right hands. In early 1995, the convention filled the sprawling Opryland Hotel in Nashville, a place that felt less like a hotel and more like a small indoor city — winding garden paths, waterfalls, glass ceilings, and thousands of people navigating the maze with badges swinging from their necks.

I was there for ministry work, not celebrity sightings. I was focused on television programming, meetings, and strategy. But as I turned a corner into one of the main exhibit halls, I saw a booth that made me stop mid-stride.

A simple table with a small stack of books and a modest sign: Rosa Parks — Quiet Strength

For a moment, the noise of the hall faded into the background.

There are some names you grow up with — names that feel almost mythic because they've been woven into the nation's memory since childhood. Rosa Parks was one of those names for me. Her act of defiance had become part of America's moral spine, a moment we all learn in school, a moment we're told changed everything.

I approached the table expecting a commanding presence — perhaps someone loud or fiery, someone who carried the weight of history with dramatic energy.

But she was the opposite.

Rosa Parks sat behind the table with hands folded loosely, a gentle smile on her face, her posture soft, steady, almost delicate. The steady flow of people approached one by one, but nothing about her demeanor suggested hurry or fatigue. She greeted each person with the same warmth, the same calm attention, the same gracious spirit.

When it was my turn, she signed a fresh copy of her book *Quiet Strength* with elegant ease. Then she looked up at me. Her voice was soft, clear.

"Thank you for coming," she said.

Four simple words. But there was weight behind them — the weight of someone who had carried history on her shoulders with dignity, not volume.

I walked away in a kind of quiet awe.

Not too long ago, I visited the Henry Ford Museum in Dearborn, Michigan. That museum is overflowing with American history — locomotives, presidential limousines, early airplanes — but nothing prepared me for the sight of that green-and-cream Montgomery city bus sitting under soft museum lights.

The bus.

The one Rosa Parks had ridden on December 1, 1955.

I climbed the steps and sat in the seat marked for visitors. The vinyl was worn smooth; the metal rails carried the subtle dents of decades of use. But what stunned me wasn't just the seat — it was the plaque.

Rosa Parks wasn't sitting in the "wrong" section.

She was in the Black section. Her seat was exactly where she was allowed to be. Exactly where she had every right to sit.

The only reason the driver demanded her seat was that the White section had filled up. Overflow meant the line of separation — the so-called "rules" — shifted backward. Again. And she was told to move so that someone else could take her rightful place.

Standing there on that bus, I realized something I had never fully grasped until that moment: This wasn't rebellion. This wasn't a noisy or dramatic explosion history sometimes paints. It was dignity. It was clarity. It was quiet conviction spoken through stillness.

She wasn't refusing to move out of the White section. She was refusing to move out of her own seat simply because injustice demanded it.

Quiet courage looks like that.

When I think back to that day in Nashville — her soft voice, her gentle posture, her steady eyes — and then to that green-and-cream bus in Dearborn, the connection becomes clear:

Rosa Parks didn't change the world because she raised her voice. She changed it because her life was aligned with her values so deeply that her stillness carried the force of an earthquake.

Quiet strength is not passive. Quiet strength is not small. It's not silent. Quiet strength is aligned … with truth, with dignity, with courage.

And alignment, more than anything else, is where real leadership draws its power.

LEADERSHIP PRINCIPLE — ALIGNMENT IS POWER

Leadership isn't tested when the cameras are rolling. It's tested in the moments when you could make a choice no one else would question — but you would.

Alignment is power. It's the difference between a leader who quietly deepens trust and a leader who slowly erodes it under their own feet. We don't fall out of alignment all at once. We leak. We compromise. We shave corners. We start telling ourselves slightly edited versions of the truth until we can no longer tell which story we're living in.

I've lived both sides of that divide — the inflated movement, the carefully framed bio, the campaign that left gaps in its own story, and the leaders who chose the harder road because they refused to break alignment with who they were. The details differ, but the pattern is the same: when the inner story and outer story diverge, everything starts to wobble.

Alignment is not perfection. It's coherence. It's integrity. It's the internal narrative matching the external one closely enough that people sense wholeness, even when they see your flaws.

And when a leader is aligned — truly aligned — something remarkable happens: their presence carries weight; their decisions earn trust; their influence deepens even without a microphone. Their legacy outlives the moment.

Because people don't follow the loudest leader, they follow the most aligned one.

THE STORY BENEATH THE STORY

For most of my life, leadership felt like something that happened outwardly — in rooms filled with people, pressure, and expectation. I learned how to shape messages that moved crowds, how to steady uncertainty when tension ran high, how to frame moments so decisions could be made and momentum could hold. Those skills mattered. They carried weight. They opened doors and sustained influence in places where clarity and confidence were not optional.

What I didn't understand for a long time was how fragile those skills become when the story beneath them begins to fracture.

The collapse of the film, the financial unraveling that followed, the months when our footing disappeared and the future narrowed to survival — none of that felt like leadership failure at first. It felt like bad timing. Bad luck. A season that would pass if I worked harder, moved faster, pushed through with enough discipline and resolve. I kept telling myself the external story was still intact, even as the internal one quietly drifted out of alignment.

That gap did not open suddenly. It widened through small accommodations — moments where momentum was allowed to speak louder than discernment, where confidence edged into performance, where the image of steadiness replaced the practice of truth. From the outside, everything still looked functional. From the inside, something was thinning.

Collapse did not create that fracture. It revealed it.

What I learned — painfully, slowly — is that a leader cannot live two competing stories for very long. One will always demand more energy than the other, and eventually the strain shows. Influence weakens. Decisions lose clarity. The steadiness others depend on begins to feel rehearsed instead of rooted. The leader becomes an interpreter of confidence rather than a carrier of truth.

The mercy of collapse is that it removes the illusion that this can continue.

In the years that followed, I watched other leaders face moments that exposed the same fault line, though the circumstances differed. Michael Brown, standing at the edge of a governor's race he had earned, chose to walk away rather than defend himself through a process that would compromise who he was. Dick Rhoads led an entire ministry with such quiet consistency that integrity never needed explanation or defense. Rosa Parks altered the course of history not through volume or spectacle, but through a stillness so aligned with truth that it could not be moved. Pat Nolan lost everything he had built, only to discover that the story God was writing ran deeper than the one he had been telling.

Different lives. Different stakes. The same underlying reality.

Where alignment exists, strength follows. Where it doesn't, no amount of skill can compensate for the fracture.

Leadership is not ultimately tested in the moments we prepare for — the speeches, the campaigns, the visible wins. It is tested in the quiet spaces where no one is watching, where the internal narrative either matches the external one or quietly contradicts it. The cost of misalignment is not immediate, but it is inevitable. And the cost of alignment, while often higher in the short term, is the only thing that sustains influence over time.

Alignment is not perfection. It's coherence. It's the ability to live one story without constant adjustment, explanation, or spin. It is the freedom that comes when a leader no longer has to protect an image because the foundation underneath it is solid.

When that coherence exists, something shifts. Presence carries weight without effort. Decisions make sense even when they are costly. Trust deepens without being requested. Influence outlives position.

People do not follow leaders because they are flawless. They follow them because they are whole.

And wholeness — in leadership, in faith, in life — is what allows a story to endure pressure without breaking. It is what gives credibility to words, steadiness to action, and meaning to sacrifice. The legacy that lasts is never built on the story we tell most convincingly, but on the one we are willing to live when the performance is stripped away.

That is the story beneath the story. And it is the one that determines whether everything else we lead can truly hold.

HOW TO APPLY THIS
LIVING ONE STORY

A NOTE ON THIS SECTION:

Parts I, II, and III focused on external leadership — how you communicate with teams and shape narratives in organizations. Part IV turns inward. These aren't tactics for managing others; they're disciplines for managing yourself. Before you can lead anyone else with integrity, you must first live with it.

Every leader eventually reaches a moment when technique stops working. The skills still function. The language still lands. The structure still holds. But something underneath has shifted. The work feels heavier. Decisions take more effort. Confidence begins to sound rehearsed, even to your own ears.

That moment is not a failure of leadership. It is often the first honest signal that the story you are living needs attention. Most leaders respond to that signal by reaching for messaging. They adjust language. They refine explanations. They polish the narrative, hoping external clarity will restore internal stability.

It won't.

Don't start with messaging. Start with meaning.

1. NAME THE FRACTURE BEFORE YOU TRY TO FIX IT

Alignment does not begin with solutions. It begins with recognition.

Slow down enough to notice where strain is actually coming from. Pay attention to the places where your public confidence no longer matches your private certainty — where momentum has begun to speak louder than conviction, where you feel yourself managing perception instead of inhabiting truth.

This kind of honesty is rarely dramatic. It looks like naming what is real without softening it, justifying it, or spinning it into something more acceptable. It means telling the truth to God without scripting the prayer. Telling the truth to the people closest to you without protecting the image you've been carrying. Telling the truth to yourself without rushing to repair it.

These moments are not indictments. They are invitations — opportunities to close a gap before pressure widens it for you.

2. REBUILD INWARD BEFORE YOU RELAUNCH OUTWARD

Reinvention is not a public act at first. It is quiet, often invisible, and almost always slower than ambition would prefer.

This is where many leaders lose patience. They attempt to rebuild too quickly, recreating the same structures that collapsed simply because they are familiar. But collapse is rarely an invitation to restore what was. It is an invitation to rebuild on something truer.

Resist the urge to announce clarity before it has settled. Let coherence return internally before you ask it to carry weight externally. Alignment formed in silence lasts longer than alignment performed in public.

3. LET YOUR LIFE REVEAL WHAT MUST CHANGE

Pay attention to what your life is already telling you.

Notice where energy drains instead of renews. Where obligations crowd out what matters most. Where success has begun to demand sacrifices that feel increasingly misaligned.

These are not inconveniences. They are indicators.

Alignment requires choosing what you will protect before ambition demands it, not after the cost has already been paid. Leadership loses its center not through one catastrophic decision, but through a series of small concessions that go unexamined.

Let your patterns speak. They are telling the truth even when your words are still polished.

4. RE-ANCHOR SPIRITUALLY BEFORE PRESSURE RETURNS

God is not a consultant waiting to endorse your next plan. He is a guide who often allows the noise to fall away so the deeper work can begin.

Spiritual alignment follows the same pattern as leadership alignment. Practices that once felt optional become essential, not as performance, but as grounding. Prayer becomes honest instead of polished. Scripture becomes confronting instead of comforting. Stillness becomes necessary instead of indulgent.

This is not withdrawal from leadership. It is preparation for a form of leadership that can withstand pressure without pretending.

As internal footing steadies, your relationship to failure changes. Mistakes no longer require explanation or concealment. They can be owned without fear because identity is no longer dependent on outcome. Integrity stops being something you project and becomes something you practice.

This is where leadership regains its weight.

Not because you have mastered a new technique — but because coherence has returned. The story you tell yourself and the story others experience begin to converge again. Presence feels grounded. Decisions feel cleaner. Influence flows not from effort, but from trust restored.

A CLOSING DISCIPLINE

Return often to places where performance is unnecessary and honesty is unavoidable.

Here is what this requires of you when no one is watching: stop rehearsing a version of yourself you can't sustain. Tell the truth before you dress it up. Let your private life catch up to your public language. Ask whether your words are rising from lived conviction or whether they are doing work your life is no longer supporting.

Protect the quiet disciplines that keep the internal story coherent — confession that is not performative, repentance that is not strategic, obedience that costs something even when no one applauds. Refuse the small concessions that slowly widen the gap between who you are and what you project.

When pressure returns, and it always does, **your leadership will not rise to the level of your messaging. It will fall back to the level of your alignment.** If the story you are living is whole, it will hold. And if it holds, others will sense it long before you ever speak.

That is how leaders endure: not by managing the story, but by living one that can carry weight, especially in the unseen places where no one is keeping score.

POSITIONING & PURPOSE: THE FORMATION OF INFLUENCE

CHAPTER 13

THE RECALL: THE WIN
YOU DON'T RECEIVE

When you've done the internal work — when you've faced failure, rebuilt faith, and reframed your story — you emerge with something most leaders lack: clarity about your true purpose.

This clarity isn't theoretical. It's forged in crisis. And it becomes the foundation for something far more powerful than ambition or strategy alone: positioning rooted in authentic purpose.

Part V explores how leaders translate internal coherence into external influence. How purpose becomes strategic positioning. And how the hardest battles sometimes position you for outcomes you couldn't have planned — outcomes that matter more than the ones you thought you were fighting for.

THE STADIUM CANDIDATE

California in 2003 felt like a state holding its breath.

The lights were flickering, literally, and the public mood carried the weight of accumulated frustration. Rolling blackouts had become a symbol of deeper instability. The budget looked like a house built on sand. Governor Gray Davis's approval numbers sank as fast as confidence in Sacramento. The recall had energy behind it, but not enough structure to turn that energy into a real political outcome.

Gubernatorial recalls happened on paper. They didn't happen in reality. Not in California. There had been 117 statewide recall attempts over the years. None ever succeeded.

But then the door opened to a different kind of moment.

Arnold Schwarzenegger stepped into the race, and the political atmosphere shifted overnight. Whatever people thought about his experience — or lack of it — his presence changed the gravitational pull of the entire recall. What had been an angry procedural effort suddenly carried the charge of entertainment, celebrity, and spectacle. Rallies no longer looked like rallies; they looked like somewhere people wanted to be.

I saw it up close. Crowds didn't just gather, they surged. Parking lots filled long before events began. Parents brought their kids because it felt like history mixed with Hollywood. Cameras didn't merely cover Schwarzenegger; they chased him like a storyline unfolding in real time.

Twisted Sister's "We're Not Gonna Take It" blasted across a sea of people that stretched far past the risers and the ropes. The song wasn't subtle, but neither was the moment. The recall, once dismissed as a political tantrum, had become a stadium tour with a candidate who understood exactly how to command a stage.

Schwarzenegger moved through the crowds with a confidence few politicians possessed. He blended humor, bravado, and unmistakable charisma. He shouted, "No more girly-men," and the crowds ate it up. The entire recall movement lifted on his shoulders.

And yet, for all the spectacle, the race carried another dimension — one that would shape the outcome far more quietly.

A dimension that lived in the margins of strategy, not in the roar of a crowd.

That dimension arrived the day the tribes called.

THE MCCLINTOCK STRATEGY

I had already done some early fundraising work for Schwarzenegger, and then I received the call: California's gaming tribes wanted to run an independent expenditure campaign to support State Senator Tom McClintock's campaign for Governor.

McClintock was a friend. He was sharp, principled, fluent in policy at a level few politicians ever achieved. His credibility was earned over years of public service. He led the fight to repeal the car tax, exposed corruption within his own party, and consistently warned about California's looming fiscal crises — often when it was politically inconvenient to do so.

But he wasn't the celebrity in the race. He didn't have the cameras. He didn't have the stadium crowds or the late-night monologues or the soundtrack of Twisted Sister following him from rally to rally.

And he didn't have the money to compete.

But the tribes? They were awash in cash.

And so, I jumped at the opportunity to head up the independent effort. But politics is rarely that simple.

I knew the tribes didn't really want Tom to become governor. They were playing me because what they wanted was far more strategic. They saw Tom as the perfect instrument to draw conservatives away from Schwarzenegger. If Tom became strong enough in the polls, the conservative base would fracture. And if that fracture widened just enough, Cruz Bustamonte, the Democratic Lieutenant Governor, could slip through the opening and become governor.

In their calculus, Tom was not a champion. He was a spoiler — a tool to weaken Arnold from the right.

I understood their logic the moment they laid out the proposal. The motives were obvious, even if not spoken aloud. Yet the opportunity still carried weight. Tom deserved to be heard. California needed the substance he brought to the conversation. If I could amplify his voice — even for reasons that made me uneasy — it could also force Arnold to take the concerns of conservatives more seriously. The tribes might have wanted Tom for one purpose, but the effect his presence would have on the broader race could be something entirely different.

I accepted the role with my eyes wide open, because this wasn't simply about what the tribes wanted. It was about what the recall itself required. And if Tom's voice could sharpen the debate and give Californians a stronger sense of what was at stake, that mattered. Even if the motivations behind the funding were more Machiavellian than noble.

Once I stepped into the independent expenditure effort, the first task was understanding where Tom stood with voters. We convened a focus group, expecting to find some combination of recognition, skepticism, and curiosity. What we found instead was far more striking. When Tom spoke — just spoke, without graphics or prompts or carefully arranged sound bites — the room grew still. Voters leaned forward. His clarity disarmed them. He didn't talk around issues; he walked through them. And people recognized the honesty in that.

It became immediately clear that the best possible advertisement was simply Tom being Tom. We didn't need slogans or orchestrated imagery. We needed to capture his authenticity on camera.

But legally, we couldn't coordinate with his campaign. We couldn't ask him to film anything. We couldn't even hint at what we needed. So we found another path.

Tom was scheduled to speak at a rally in Southern California, and we requested press credentials, showing up with a full crew and treating the event as if we were covering it for the evening news. We filmed everything — his arrival, his conversations with supporters, the way he gestured when explaining something complicated, the quiet confidence that came through when he spoke from conviction rather than performance.

By the time we packed up our equipment, we had all the footage we would ever need.

The edit that followed was simple but powerful: Tom speaking directly to Californians, on his own terms, in his own voice.

Then came the strategic crossroads.

We had a couple of million dollars to spend — enough to make an impact, but not enough to cover the entire state. The obvious move, the safe move, was Northern California. The markets were cheaper, the conservative base stronger, and Tom's message would resonate quickly and easily. We could saturate the airwaves and make a real dent. The representative for the tribes pushed for this, but I believed the recall itself was going to rise or fall in Southern California.

Los Angeles and San Diego were expensive, crowded, chaotic media environments. They were also where millions of voters were barely paying attention — voters who could be swayed by a clear, steady voice that broke through the noise. Tom would not have the budget to compete here, but if his message reached them, two things could happen at once: the recall could gather strength among conservatives who needed a reason to engage, and Schwarzenegger could feel the pressure to shore up his right flank. Both outcomes mattered, even if they moved in different political directions.

What the tribes wanted and what the movement needed were not the same thing, but the geography for both pointed to the same place.

So we committed the budget to Southern California.

We purchased time in Los Angeles and San Diego, placing Tom McClintock — an unvarnished, unflinching truth-teller — directly in front of millions of voters who had never heard him before. The choice was bold and risky, but it was also strategically pure. Northern California would have been easy. Southern California was consequential.

As the ads rolled out, something remarkable began to happen. Tom's numbers did climb, but not in a way that threatened to put him in the governor's office. Instead, his rise created a gravitational pull that shifted the entire race. Schwarzenegger, sensing the movement among conservatives, began adjusting his rhetoric — first subtly, then more directly. Themes of reform, fiscal responsibility, and "blowing up the boxes" emerged where they had been vague before. Arnold wasn't losing the race to Tom, but he was being shaped by him.

The tribes wanted Tom to drain votes from Arnold. They didn't expect Tom to change him.

But that's the thing about narrative gravity: once it takes hold, it doesn't always obey the intentions of the people who set it in motion. Tom didn't become governor, but he changed the direction of the race. He sharpened the debate. He forced California to hear what it had been ignoring. And he nudged Schwarzenegger toward the right at the precise moment conservatives needed reassurance.

Tom didn't become governor, but he changed the direction of the race.

The tribes funded a spoiler. What they got was a compass.

And as the recall approached its climax, the influence of that compass became impossible to ignore.

WHEN INFLUENCE ISN'T VISIBLE

Election night in California felt like the end of a storm. For weeks, the state had been caught in a political whirlwind — rallies, arguments, late-night strategy sessions, and the strange exhilaration of watching history unfold in real time. When the results became clear, the headline was unmistakable: the recall had succeeded. For the first time in California's history, voters had removed a sitting governor at the ballot box. And Arnold Schwarzenegger, the global celebrity who had turned politics into something that felt like a summer blockbuster, had won the governorship.

Almost immediately, the narrative settled into place. The cameras focused on Arnold. The commentators focused on Arnold. The photographs, the analysis, the late-night monologues — everything gravitated toward the new governor who now dominated the frame. Tom McClintock's name barely registered in the national conversation. His presence felt like a footnote, an honorable mention, a detail from a subplot in someone else's movie.

But politics doesn't end when the cameras turn off. The truth of an election rarely reveals itself in the headlines.

Post-election analysis — both ours internally and from outside observers — showed something striking: McClintock's vote total was larger than the margin by which Davis was recalled. In other words, if even a fraction of his voters had stayed home, the recall itself likely would have failed.

Our ads had reached voters who otherwise would have stayed home. Tom's credibility grounded a race that could easily have drifted into pure entertainment. Tom's presence attracted precisely the voters who might have rolled their eyes at a Hollywood candidate leading a statewide revolution.

Tom didn't win the governorship. But he created the conditions that made victory possible for someone else. He altered the gravitational field of the entire election without ever standing in the center of the frame. And watching that truth unfold taught me one of the most important lessons of influence I have ever carried into leadership, politics, or life:

Not every decisive force is visible. Some forms of impact only appear in the aftermath — revealed not by applause, but by analysis.

Not every decisive force is visible.

THE CALIFORNIA REPUBLICAN ASSEMBLY

By the time the recall gathered the full force of its momentum, another shift was happening inside the conservative movement — one that would come to shape the environment I was working in just as profoundly as the campaigns on the ballot. Mike Spence had just been elected President of the California Republican Assembly, and although I knew him only in passing at the time, that changed almost instantly.

Mike was one of those rare political figures who combined an encyclopedic memory with a razor-dry sense of humor. He looked like someone you might pass in a grocery store without noticing — until he started talking. Then you realized you were dealing with one of the brightest political minds in the state. His wit could be sharp, and behind every joke was a mind processing layers of context faster than most people could follow.

When he asked to meet shortly after his election, I assumed it would be a standard transition conversation: goals, structure, messaging. Instead, we spent hours talking, laughing, strategizing, and discovering that we viewed movement-building almost identically. By the end of that meeting, the partnership had already formed. We didn't declare it. We just started working together as if it were the most natural thing in the world.

CRA, the "conscience of the Republican Party," as Ronald Reagan called it, had a long, proud history. But like many volunteer organizations, its numbers had ebbed and flowed over the decades. By the early 2000s, membership had dipped, chapters varied widely in strength, and opponents often dismissed CRA as a relic of earlier conservative cycles. What I understood, and what Mike instinctively knew as well, was that perception mattered just as much as reality. And in California politics, perception often was reality.

Our goal wasn't to inflate CRA's importance. It was to remind Sacramento of the influence it already had when fully mobilized. But to do that, we had to rebuild the organization's presence in a way that made it impossible to ignore.

So we leaned into what I knew best: communication.

Every month, we printed *The California Republican,* CRA's flagship newspaper, and we widened its reach dramatically. Instead of limiting it to dues-paying members, we sent it to every Republican legislator, both at the Capitol and in their district offices. We blanketed media outlets up and down the state: political reporters, editorial boards, talk radio hosts, local columnists. We made sure that when CRA endorsed a candidate or took a stand, the people who needed to notice actually did.

And we started building our presence on the Internet, and through email. Slowly, almost imperceptibly at first, something shifted.

Legislators who had once dismissed the organization began calling Mike for meetings. Consultants who claimed CRA was irrelevant started asking when endorsements would be considered. Journalists began quoting our statements again, framing CRA positions as indicators of where grassroots conservatives stood. It wasn't magic, and it wasn't manipulation. It was the deliberate restoration of a movement's voice.

Mike and I understood that movements survive on narrative coherence. When people believe an organization is strong, unified, and principled, they engage with it differently. They listen. They adjust. They take it seriously. And in political ecosystems as complex as California's, even a small shift in perceived power can change the gravitational pull of an entire cycle.

During and after the recall, that narrative gravity mattered. CRA endorsements rippled outward. Our newspaper shaped conversations in offices we never set foot in. And our websites — ShelleyMustResign.com, SaveOurLicense.com, BeatBoxer.com — gained traction.

Because Mike and I sustained the illusion of a large, mobilized grassroots army, many campaigns — and not a few legislators — calculated their decisions with CRA in mind.

The truth is that CRA's real strength wasn't in numbers. It was in positioning.

By rebuilding its presence statewide, we placed CRA back into the political orbit where it had once lived comfortably. And in a chaotic election defined by celebrity, fragmentation, and strategic gambits, that positioning gave the movement a weight it hadn't carried in years.

Looking back, it's clear that we weren't just running a volunteer organization.

We were shaping the environment in which the entire recall played out — quietly, steadily, from just outside the center of the frame.

And in that environment, the smallest shift in gravity could change the outcome of the entire race.

WHEN A MOVEMENT FORGETS ITS OWN STORY

For several years, the momentum inside CRA held. Legislators called. Consultants recalibrated. Reporters watched our statements the way they once watched polling data. The organization felt bigger than it was because the story we projected matched the seriousness with which we carried the work.

But movements do not stay in the hands of any leader forever.

After Mike completed his final term as president, a new team stepped in — well-intentioned, earnest, determined to "clean things up." They inherited a movement that had regained relevance, but they misunderstood what had created that relevance in the first place.

They looked at CRA through a purely administrative lens.

Lists were audited. Names were purged. chapters that couldn't produce perfect paperwork were closed. Energy that had once gone into presence, momentum, and messaging now went into compliance, technicalities, and internal policing.

They cared about accuracy. They cared about order. But they didn't understand narrative gravity — the invisible force that had made CRA matter again.

In trying to make the organization more "honest," they unintentionally made it smaller.

Legislators stopped calling. Consultants stopped watching. Reporters stopped quoting. And the statewide influence CRA had rebuilt — fragile, hard-won, and more dependent on story than on structure — evaporated with stunning speed.

The organization still exists. Its people still care deeply. But the narrative weight it once carried has never returned to what it was in the Spence years.

That period became one of the most sobering leadership lessons I ever witnessed: A movement can survive imperfect paperwork. It cannot survive a broken story.

Because in the end, others take their cues not from your technical accuracy, but from the narrative they believe you are living.

A movement can survive imperfect paperwork. It cannot survive a broken story.

CHAPTER 14

INFLUENCE FROM
OUTSIDE THE FRAME

Influence is often misunderstood. We tend to assume it belongs to the person bathed in light, the figure at the podium, the one who claims the microphone or appears in the headline. But leadership rarely confines itself to the center of the photograph. History is filled with moments where the decisive force came not from the most prominent voice in the room, but from someone standing just outside the frame — quietly, deliberately shaping the conditions in which the visible leader operates.

Positioning, in that sense, is its own form of power.

Positioning is its own form of power.

It is the ability to see the full landscape of a moment, to understand where someone must stand for their presence to matter most, and to place them there with clarity and purpose. It's the recognition that the right influence at the right time can redirect an entire narrative, even when the person exercising that influence never walks onto the main stage.

The recall demonstrated this principle perfectly.

Arnold Schwarzenegger won the governorship. He became the story, the symbol, the image that defined the election. But beneath that highly produced surface, Tom McClintock quietly altered the gravitational pull of the race. His presence strengthened conservative turnout. His seriousness stabilized a process that could easily have devolved into entertainment. His rising numbers shifted Schwarzenegger's rhetoric rightward at a moment when the campaign desperately needed grounding.

Tom didn't take the oath of office, but he shaped the environment in which another man did.

And then there was the influence that lived even further outside the spotlight — inside the California Republican Assembly. When Mike Spence and I rebuilt CRA's presence statewide, we weren't trying to inflate its importance; we were reestablishing its narrative weight. By restoring its voice in legislative offices, by ensuring our message reached power centers across California, by projecting an image of unity and movement even when the organization was rebuilding its footing, we positioned CRA as a gravitational actor during the recall, a force campaigns had to account for even if they didn't fully understand its inner workings.

That is the essence of strategic positioning.

It isn't manipulation, and it isn't sleight of hand. It is the disciplined art of understanding the stage deeply enough to know where influence actually lives — and then placing people and movements where their presence will create the greatest impact.

Leadership doesn't always announce itself from the spotlight. More often, it works from the edges, from the places where framing happens and momentum is shaped. It lives in the voices that steady a chaotic moment, in the organizations that reassert their identity, in the candidates whose clarity alters the trajectory of a race even when they don't win it.

Influence, at its most powerful, is rarely loud. It is rarely obvious. It is rarely credited.

But when used with purpose, it can shift the direction of an entire movement.

Strategic positioning is the leadership skill that allows you not just to see the story unfolding, but to understand where you — or someone you champion — must stand to change it. It is one of the rarest and most sophisticated forms of leadership there is, because it demands humility, clarity, foresight, and an instinct for how narrative truly works.

And as the recall taught me, the person who reshapes the story is often not the one in the spotlight at all — but the one who understands the frame.

The person who reshapes the story is often not the one in the spotlight.

REBRANDING A MOVEMENT

I came to the California Republican Assembly almost by accident. CRA was, at that time, both legendary and wounded. It was the oldest conservative grassroots organization in the state, the "conscience of the Republican Party," as Reagan called it, but its influence had ebbed and flowed across the decades. By the early nineties, it was beginning to stir again. A new generation was emerging, angling to rebuild the movement's credibility and restore the storytelling power it had once possessed.

One of those new voices was Greg Hardcastle.

Greg had just been elected state president. He was disciplined, principled, and effective, and as President of the Sacramento chapter, had played a key role in helping David Knowles get elected to the Legislature. His election to state President marked a turning point. CRA wasn't just electing officers; it was choosing a direction. It wanted relevance again. It wanted definition again. And more than anything, it wanted a story that matched the seriousness of its mission.

That's when Pam Ross entered the picture.

Pam was smart, perceptive, and fiercely committed to the movement. She had just stepped in as editor of the organization's longtime newsletter, *CRA News*, and she reached out to me for help.

We spent an afternoon brainstorming, and I suggested a complete rebranding — everything from the name to the logo and the layout. A movement's publication, I argued, should reflect its identity, its confidence, and its aspirations. If CRA was finding its voice again, its newspaper needed to speak clearly.

She agreed and we set to work.

We looked back at the organization's early days — the founding years, the fights, the faces, the moments when CRA had shaped statewide direction. Buried in that history, we discovered a name the group had used decades earlier: *The California Republican*.

The more we said it out loud, the more it felt like reclaiming something essential.

So we brought it back.

In 1993, we retired the familiar but limited *CRA News* and relaunched the publication under its historic banner. We rebuilt the layout, the masthead, the visual identity. We expanded the content. The new name carried weight — geographic, political, emotional. It sounded like a movement with confidence, not a club sending updates.

But the change was deeper than ink or typography. It was a shift in narrative posture.

Movements live or die on the stories they tell about themselves. A fractured movement tells a fractured story. A rising movement tells a story with momentum, coherence, and purpose. With Greg at the helm and Pam shaping the editorial voice, the paper became a mirror through which CRA could see itself not as a relic, but as a force — an organization with history, influence, and clarity.

For the next several years, I designed and produced every issue. Each edition that went to press felt like placing another brick in a rebuilt foundation. We weren't simply reporting what happened at meetings or conventions. We were shaping identity — reminding members who they were, what they stood for, and why their voice still mattered in a state that often told them it didn't. When Pam stepped down, I stepped up and continued in the role as Editor and Publisher for another decade.

Looking back, those years were my apprenticeship in movement narrative. I learned that organizations don't rise because they are large or rich or well-connected. They rise when they reclaim the story that gives them purpose. They rise when they frame themselves not around nostalgia or grievance, but around conviction and mission.

CRA didn't become perfect during those years. But it became clearer. Stronger. More unified. It found its voice again. And in helping rebrand that movement, I discovered something about leadership that I would carry with me into every campaign, crisis, and crucible that followed:

The story a movement tells about itself determines whether it advances or disappears.

Narrative is not decoration. Narrative is direction.

THE DAY-ONE RESET

Understanding positioning isn't limited to external campaigns or public narratives. Sometimes the most important positioning happens internally — when a leader establishes the ground rules that will define an organization's culture for years to come.

Shortly before I moved to California, Pat Nolan was elected Assembly

Republican Leader in the California Legislature — a moment that signaled a significant change in both policy and internal direction. His first act in office sent a message no one misunderstood. On day one, he released the entire support staff — every aide, every analyst, every administrator — and invited each of them to reapply for their positions. No automatic carryovers. No protected roles. No assumptions.

From the outside, it looked abrupt, even severe. But it was something far more intentional. It wasn't retaliation or theatrics. It was a reset — a way to ensure that the team moving forward would be both effective and aligned. In the political world, divided loyalties can quietly derail momentum. Pat understood that. By requiring every staff member to step forward again, he made two things unmistakably clear: competence mattered, and loyalty mattered.

Without a speech or a slogan, he communicated that a new culture was beginning — one where clarity of mission and unity of purpose were non-negotiable. It was his way of saying, "There's a new sheriff in town," without ever needing to use the words.

He wasn't simply rehiring staff. He was establishing authority, elevating standards, and building a framework strong enough to hold the work ahead.

SAVE OUR LICENSE

If the recall taught me that positioning could change a statewide election, the "Save Our License" fight proved that it could bend the legislature itself.

In 2003, not long after the recall machinery began humming, Governor Gray Davis signed SB60 — a bill that would grant driver's licenses to illegal immigrants. It wasn't a symbolic gesture. It was the kind of legislative shift that could alter voter rolls, reshape law enforcement protocols, and send a signal far beyond Sacramento. The political world understood the implications immediately. So did the grassroots.

CRA responded the only way a movement like ours knew how: fast, direct, and without hesitation. Mike Spence mobilized chapters across the state, and together we launched a referendum to overturn the law. The task was enormous. We had a narrow window to gather more than half a million valid signatures — an effort that required volunteers in parking lots, church foyers, farmers' markets, and every suburban sidewalk in between.

As the petition drive gained traction, the media took notice. Conservative talk radio lit up. Local news stations began running stories about the growing backlash. Reporters who had long ignored CRA suddenly treated the organization like the pulse of the grassroots. And the legislature started to worry — not because we had the signatures, but because they feared we might.

That fear became the one piece of leverage we needed.

Mike, ever calm and sharp, found himself summoned to a legislative hearing where lawmakers grilled him about the referendum's progress. Their questions came rapid-fire — how many signatures, how many counties, how many volunteers, how close were we? What they were really asking was far simpler: Are we in trouble?

Mike knew the truth. We were close, but not close enough. We didn't yet have the signatures required to force the referendum onto the ballot, and we likely would not make it.

But here's where positioning once again proved decisive.

Mike didn't lie. He didn't inflate numbers. He didn't boast. He simply refused to give the legislature the comfort of certainty. He let them sit with the possibility, just the possibility, that we might succeed. He let the tension breathe. The ambiguity worked on them harder than any statistic could have.

The legislature panicked.

In a move so unprecedented it barely seemed real at the time, they voted to repeal the law themselves — before it took effect. SB60 became the first bill in California history repealed prior to implementation, undone not by an election, not by a court ruling, but by the perceived momentum of a grassroots army the legislature wasn't willing to gamble against.

The bluff worked because it wasn't truly a bluff. The momentum was real — even if our signature count was still short. The movement felt strong. The media believed it was strong. The legislators feared it was strong. And in politics, fear is often more powerful than fact.

What mattered wasn't the signature total. What mattered was the narrative of inevitability.

The same principle that had shaped the recall — positioning, perception, gravitational influence — was at work here too. When people believe a force is rising, they behave differently. They hedge. They retreat. They make decisions based on what might be true rather than what they can verify.

And in that moment, positioning didn't just influence an election. It rewrote a law.

This was leadership from the edges once more — where the outcome is changed not by the biggest voice in the room, but by the quiet confidence of a movement that understood its power long before others recognized it.

CHAPTER 15

CFAN: PURPOSE AS STRATEGIC POSITIONING

The recall and the CRA battles taught me how positioning works in political ecosystems — how perception shapes reality, how narrative creates gravity. But the deepest lessons about positioning came from a world far removed from California campaigns. They came from a different kind of leadership — one built on mission, faith, and global perspective.

Losing my position in the California Legislature was one of those blows you don't fully feel until long after the moment has passed. After helping elect David Knowles to the State Assembly in 1990, I became his Chief of Staff, stepping into a role I admired but wasn't entirely ready for. The strategic parts of the job energized me — the framing of legislation, the shaping of messages, the political storytelling that lifted complicated issues into clarity. But the day-to-day machinery of staff management, scheduling, and procedural detail never matched my wiring. We accomplished meaningful work together, but I failed David in ways I still regret.

After managing his successful 1992 re-election campaign, I expected to return to the Capitol with renewed purpose. Instead, I walked into a perfect storm: California's new term limits law slashed the legislative budget, and as an "at-will" employee with one of the higher salaries, I became an easy cut. David let me go. I understood why. That didn't soften the sting.

The irony was that my future had already taken root months earlier without me realizing it. During the campaign, I produced a light-hearted video for David's 40th birthday — old photos, interviews with friends and family, humor — something that showed a side of him voters rarely saw. We screened it at a fundraiser, and it landed beautifully. I didn't yet understand that I had just glimpsed the next chapter of my life.

After leaving the legislature, I was approached by the Executive Director of Gun Owners of California. The organization had been founded by Senator H.L.

"Bill" Richardson, who also ran Red Barn Video, a small production house that needed revitalizing. They offered me the chance to run it.

Suddenly, I found myself with a broadcast-quality Betacam camera, a digital effects system, a fully outfitted editing bay, and a massive archive of footage — tools I had never imagined I would have access to. I dove into producing documentary-style pieces for Gun Owners of California, Gun Owners of America, and even Assemblyman Knowles. I produced a television spot for the Sacramento District Attorney's race and crafted a promotional video for a small company called Regulok.

It was creative work, fulfilling work, and occasionally it even paid well. But it was also unpredictable — an exhausting dance between overflowing projects and weeks of silence. Supporting a young family on feast-or-famine freelance work took its toll. I enjoyed the craft, but I could feel that I was missing something — direction, stability, purpose.

Then an unexpected door opened.

A friend told me that Reinhard Bonnke Ministries, the U.S. arm of Christ for All Nations (CfaN), was looking for someone who could handle their design and communications. I had heard Bonnke's name, but only faintly. I knew nothing of the massive crusades he led, the crowds he preached to, or the reach of his ministry. Before making any decision, I called a pastor friend for counsel.

He didn't hesitate.

"Of all the ministries out there," he said, "Bonnke's is the one I trust. The word that comes to mind is integrity."

In an era still shaking from the scandals of the Bakers, Swaggart, and others, integrity was not a word I took lightly. I met with the U.S. Director, Ron Shaw, and before long I stepped into the role of CfaN's Media Director.

I didn't know it then, but this was the beginning of the most transformative five-year stretch of my life.

A MAN OF ONE PURPOSE

Working for Reinhard Bonnke was unlike anything I had ever experienced in politics or production. He carried a single-minded devotion that didn't fluctuate with circumstances or audiences. His purpose was to reach the lost, and everything in his life orbited that calling. It wasn't branding. It wasn't rhetoric. It was the internal fire that shaped every decision he made.

Bonnke had the intensity of a man who knew exactly why he was alive. When you talked to him about logistics, he asked how it helped reach the lost. When you talked about budgets, he asked whether money was being stewarded toward souls. When you talked about travel, storms, setbacks, or strategy, his question always carried the same gravitational pull. Purpose clarified everything.

And yet behind the boldness was a surprising gentleness. Offstage, Bonnke was humble, warm, almost soft-spoken. He prayed easily, laughed quickly, and carried no pretense. You never felt like you were working for a celebrity evangelist. You felt like you were standing beside a man convinced that God had given him an assignment too urgent for hesitation.

He lived in two modes: clarity and compassion. The clarity drove the mission. The compassion fueled the man. It was why he could preach to a million people at night and spend the next morning in deep, quiet prayer. His focus never diminished his tenderness.

Purpose clarified everything.

Being around him recalibrated something in me. In politics, purpose is often negotiated. With Bonnke, purpose was oxygen. It animated him. It steadied him. And it reminded everyone around him that influence means nothing if it isn't anchored in calling.

BUILDING STORIES FOR A MOVEMENT

My role began with the direct mail program, but Ron Shaw quickly expanded my responsibilities. He had a renewed vision for CfaN's weekly television program — a broadcast that had once carried the ministry's stories, miracles, and crusade moments into living rooms across America. If CfaN was going to reach the next generation, the program had to be reborn, not just resumed.

To help us do it, we brought in Craig Forrest — a seasoned storyteller with the dust of dozens of nations on his boots. Craig was the kind of producer who could film a refugee camp in the morning, a cathedral in the afternoon, and a crusade of 500,000 that night, all without losing the emotional thread. He had worked in war zones, jungles, remote villages, deserts, and megacities. Wherever people were hurting or hoping, Craig had found a way to frame it with dignity.

Under his direction, we began sifting through years of crusade footage.

Together, we built a new series from the ground up and relaunched it on the Trinity Broadcasting Network (TBN), where it reached millions of viewers each week. It felt like rediscovering the ministry's heartbeat through a camera lens.

And then the travel began. I didn't know it then, but that first trip would reshape everything I thought I understood about leadership, influence, and the kind of power that actually changes lives.

CHAPTER 16

WHEN PURPOSE MEETS CRISIS

My first overseas trip for CfaN was to Addis Ababa, Ethiopia. I traveled with Ron and Craig — two men who, in their differences, embodied a kind of balanced leadership I had rarely seen. Ron had the presence of a seasoned pastor: calm, relational, unhurried even under pressure. Craig was precise, observant, always scanning a room for light, angle, or risk. Together they created a strange sense of safety, as if their steadiness could insulate us from the unpredictability around us. We joined the rest of the CfaN team and set about doing our work.

One of our filming days took us to a leper colony outside the city. The approach alone felt tense. Eyes followed us from the moment our vehicle rolled to a stop — curious, cautious, and in some cases openly hostile. Cameras can be a bridge or a barrier, and here they were definitely the latter.

As Craig lifted his camera to frame a shot, something whizzed past me — an apple, thrown with force, striking the base of his neck. I flinched. Craig didn't. He didn't even turn to look. He steadied the camera, made a micro-adjustment, and kept filming. No anger or reaction. Just a quiet, unspoken acknowledgment that documenting pain sometimes meant absorbing some of it. It was professionalism, but it was also something deeper — a commitment to bear witness without inserting himself into the moment.

But the bigger crisis was unfolding miles away.

CfaN had planned a massive gospel crusade on the outskirts of the city — months of coordination with local churches, government permits secured, transportation arranged, prayer teams mobilized, every logistical thread meticulously tightened. Hundreds of thousands were expected.

Then Ethiopia's Orthodox Church intervened.

Word spread quickly: priests and adherents were marching toward the crusade grounds. By midday, the protest became a riot. Police responded. Chaos erupted. And within hours, the government cancelled the entire event, declaring it too dangerous to proceed.

In the world I came from, a cancellation like that wasn't just a setback — it was a collapse. Months of work erased. Budgets exploded. Narratives imploded. Reputations suffered.

But CfaN didn't panic.

No frantic emergency meetings. No blame or despair. Just a quiet pivot, almost like they'd been expecting it.

Within hours, the team restructured the entire mission. Instead of a city-wide crusade, they organized a weeklong "Fire Conference" — a gathering for pastors, leaders, and church workers from across Ethiopia. Tents went up at a church compound. Word spread through local networks. And by morning, hundreds poured in.

For seven straight days, Reinhard Bonnke preached with the same passion he would have brought to a field of 100,000. No disappointment or diminished fire. He thundered about the Gospel with the intensity of a man who didn't measure impact by crowd size.

Meanwhile, our afternoons were spent at the Hilton — a surreal contrast that still makes me smile. Outside, tension simmered. Inside, we ate by the pool, played a round of mini-golf, answered emails from frantic colleagues who were sure we were in danger. It was like living in two worlds at once: turbulence and tranquility, risk and rest.

But even that contrast held a lesson.

CfaN wasn't in Ethiopia to execute a plan. They were there to fulfill a mission. If the circumstances changed, the mission didn't. Purpose gave them flexibility, not fragility. They weren't undone by the cancelled event because the cancelled event wasn't the point.

It took me years to fully recognize it, but that week in Ethiopia taught me something about leadership that politics never could:

When purpose is clear, positioning is effortless. When mission is fixed, method becomes adaptable. And when calling is your center of gravity, nothing — not riots, not cancelled events, not thrown apples — knocks you off course.

This was purpose distilled. Purpose embodied. Purpose as the ultimate form of positioning.

When purpose is clear, positioning is effortless.

INDIA: WHEN NARRATIVE BREAKS YOU

If Ethiopia taught me how purpose handles crisis, India would show me how purpose builds legacy.

CfaN's work had expanded into India, largely because of Ron Shaw. It was his country of birth, his old mission field, and the place where he had poured years of his life into students, families, and a city that seemed to recognize him on sight. The ministry had just completed a successful crusade in Madras, now Chennai, and the momentum opened doors across the subcontinent. The following year, Ron invited me to travel with him for three weeks — two spent crisscrossing India with a camera on my shoulder, gathering stories; the third in Bangalore, where a massive gospel crusade would close the journey.

India does not ease you in. From the moment we stepped into New Delhi, it felt as though the volume of the world had been turned up. Horns blared in every direction. Voices layered on top of one another in markets that seemed to spill into the streets. The air carried curry, exhaust, smoke, and something harder to name — the smell of strain, of too many people fighting for too little space. Poverty wasn't hidden; it sat in doorways and slept on sidewalks, wove itself into traffic and pressed against bus windows.

We gathered footage in the city — Hindu temples, snake charmers, historic forts — and we made a visit to Agra to film the Taj Mahal.

After Delhi, we landed in Calcutta and made our way to the Assembly of God church compound, the place where Ron had once spent years serving under the ministry founded by Mark and Huldah Buntain. It wasn't a single building but an entire ecosystem of ministry woven into the heart of Calcutta. The compound sat just off a crowded street where rickshaws, scooters, and pedestrians flowed in a steady, unbroken current. From the outside, it looked like part of the city's natural architecture — concrete walls softened by age, gates that never fully closed, and a steady stream of people moving in and out.

But once you stepped inside, it felt different.

The noise of the street didn't disappear, but it softened, absorbed into the courtyards and open walkways that connected each part of the ministry. Children in crisp school uniforms hurried between classes, their laughter bouncing off the long, sun-washed corridors of the AG Church School. Teachers stood in doorways calling out instructions; older students lingered beneath archways with notebooks in hand. The school itself stretched across multiple levels, a labyrinth of classrooms stacked above one another with railings overlooking the main courtyard.

Everywhere we walked, people greeted Ron as if a local celebrity had returned. Men crossed the street to shake his hand. Mothers stepped forward and introduced their children. Shopkeepers left their counters just long enough to say hello.

"Doctor Shaw, do you remember me?"

"Sir, my son graduated from your school."

"Sir, because of you, I became a teacher."

It was that school that had written Ron's name into the fabric of Calcutta. Years earlier, he had served as principal and superintendent. Thousands of first-generation students had passed through those classrooms. It was their gratitude that chased him down the street.

Watching that, I realized I wasn't looking at celebrity. I was looking at legacy.

We walked the corridors while Ron pointed out classrooms and staff members, sharing stories of former students now scattered throughout the city in careers they never would have imagined without an education. Then he gestured toward another part of the compound.

"And here's the hospital," he said casually.

Ron had often told me of the hospital he and his wife, Felicia, had built. When someone tells you they helped build a hospital in India, you picture something modest — a clinic, maybe a one-story building with a few exam rooms and some crowded wards. That's what I expected.

Instead, the skyline opened up and there it was: a six-story hospital rising above the neighborhood, with 250 beds, surgical theaters, and an intensive care unit. Nurses in white sarees moved through the entryway. Families sat on steps waiting for visiting hours. It looked like a mid-sized American hospital had been quietly dropped into the middle of Calcutta.

I remember stopping mid-step, trying to reconcile what I was seeing with the matter-of-fact way Ron had mentioned it.

It struck me that some leaders shout their accomplishments into microphones. Others just build hospitals and move on.

We toured the grounds, moving from the hospital back through the school, past students laughing in courtyards and teachers carrying stacks of papers. The compound hummed with life. And with every greeting, every handshake, every "Doctor Shaw, do you remember me?," the picture came into focus. Ron's influence in Calcutta didn't rest on a title. It rested on years of steady presence. This was what quiet power looked like: not a platform, but a footprint.

MOTHER TERESA

Later that afternoon, we stepped into the church offices, a simple space where staff moved quietly between desks and filing cabinets.

"Let's see if Mother Teresa is available," Ron exclaimed.

The secretary picked up the phone, dialed a number, and said, "Hello, Mother. I have Doctor Shaw here with a guest. Yes... yes... I'll send them over."

She hung up as if she'd just confirmed a lunch order.

I looked at Ron. "That's it?"

He smiled. "We're nearby. She is kind."

Her office wasn't far — a modest concrete building with a second-floor walkway and a wooden bench just outside her door. There were no security details, or metal detectors, or velvet ropes, or PR staff arranging the moment. We sat on the bench and waited while the sounds of the city drifted up from below.

A minute later, she appeared.

She was smaller than I expected, wrapped in the familiar white sari with blue trim, moving with a careful, deliberate gait. There was nothing dramatic about her entrance. And yet the air around her felt different, weighted with something that can only be described as moral gravity.

Ron and I stood and greeted her. She took his hands like an old friend. Then her eyes moved to me and to the big camera slung over my shoulder. She smiled gently and said, "No video today."

We sat on the bench, and she settled in beside me, close enough that I could hear the faint rustle of fabric when she shifted. Her voice was softer than I imagined. I had to lean in, closer than felt entirely comfortable, just to catch each sentence.

She asked about our work in India, about the ministry, about the people we were filming. When Ron mentioned the hospital on the church grounds, she nodded and said, almost to herself, "It's such a blessing. The work never ends."

The work never ends.

It was the kind of line that could sound cliche in the wrong mouth, but coming from her — someone who had spent decades in the trenches of human suffering — it felt less like a statement and more like a diagnosis. She wasn't complaining. She was simply describing reality. The needs were unending. The calling had to be, too.

Later, as we walked back through the streets, Ron told me more stories about her. He described the day he and a wealthy businessman had waited for an appointment, only to see her approaching on foot, weaving through traffic with the calm of someone utterly unconcerned with her own comfort. When the businessman asked why she hadn't taken a taxi or rickshaw, which was so convenient, she simply replied, "I took a vow of poverty, not of convenience."

On another occasion, a businessman arrived radiating his own success, talking at length about how well his company had done before finally handing her a sizable check. She accepted it, looked at it for a moment, then handed it back and said, "You should give out of your poverty, not your prosperity."

Neither story was delivered with drama, but each one revealed a woman whose life was so aligned with her values that even her smallest choices became instruction.

Sitting with her that day, listening to her barely audible questions and simple observations, I realized she didn't lead because the world listened to her voice. She led because the world recognized her life. Her story was the megaphone. Her choices were the message. Her sacrifices were the sermon.

Ethiopia had shown me how purpose can hold steady in crisis. Calcutta showed me something deeper: that true influence doesn't need volume. It needs alignment.

We left her office, stepped back into the roaring rhythm of the city — horns, shouts, bicycle bells, vendors calling out their wares — and walked toward the next flight, the next city, the next story. But inside, something had stilled. The noise outside hadn't changed. The internal noise had.

Her story was the megaphone.

Later, in Bangalore, I would stand on a camera platform and watch as nearly 150,000 people gathered each night to hear Bonnke preach. I would see families respond together, tears on faces that had seen more hardship than I could imagine. I would watch Governor H. D. Deve Gowda — soon to be Prime Minister — step onto a crusade platform to offer a public blessing over meetings led by a German evangelist whose only real credential in that country was integrity.

By the time that trip ended, I understood that what I was seeing in India and Ethiopia and places like Calcutta wasn't separate from what I had learned in politics. It was a deeper layer of the same truth.

Positioning matters — but not just on a stage or in a strategy. It matters in life.

The leaders who move the world are not always the ones with microphones or headlines. Often, they are the ones who walk barefoot when convenience is an option, who build schools and hospitals without bragging about it, who whisper truths that reshape the people close enough to hear.

QUIET POWER. HUMILITY, CONVICTION, SACRIFICE.

Looking back, India gave me a new understanding of leadership that would follow me back into politics and into every room where influence and story and responsibility collide.

And it all began with a school in Calcutta, a hospital I never expected, and a whispered conversation on a wooden bench outside a small office with a woman the world called a saint — but who seemed far more interested in the work that never ends than in any title she'd ever been given.

THE INVISIBLE GRAVITY OF INFLUENCE

When I remember the 2003 recall as it happened, the images come back loud.

Parking lots filling early. Music thundering across crowds. Cameras chasing Arnold like he was a storyline, not a candidate. The whole state felt like it had been pulled into a spectacle big enough to rearrange reality.

But when time gives you distance, the recall changes shape. The stadium atmosphere fades, and what remains is something quieter — a lesson about influence that has almost nothing to do with who held the microphone.

Because **the decisive forces in that election were not always the ones bathed in light.**

Arnold became the headline, the symbol, the face that history chose to remember. But the recall was steadied, in part, by a man who never touched the governor's chair. Tom McClintock was not the center of the frame. He didn't have celebrity gravity. He didn't have the soundtrack. What he had was something rarer in politics: seriousness without theatrics, conviction without performance. He held a posture that made the moment feel real again — and that posture altered the environment around him.

Not by winning.

By shifting what everyone else had to account for.

And that is where positioning begins to reveal its true meaning. It isn't "branding." It isn't clever framing. It's not manipulation of perception. It's the choice of ground — the place you decide to stand when you could take easier ground, louder ground, safer ground, or more flattering ground.

McClintock's presence did not take the office. It changed the conditions under which another man could.

Later, the analysis made it plain: his vote total mattered more than anyone wanted to admit in the victory narrative. The recall was celebrated as Arnold's triumph. But beneath that surface was a quieter truth — that turnout, seriousness, and conservative engagement had been shaped by a candidate most people treated like a subplot.

Influence is often like that. It operates in the margins. It does its work in the background. It reshapes outcomes without receiving credit.

I saw the same principle again through CRA. We didn't create power out of thin air. We restored presence — consistent communication, a regained voice, a reasserted story. And once that story had weight again, lawmakers and consultants began behaving differently, not because they had suddenly fallen in love with the organization, but because they could feel its gravity returning.

People act differently when they believe something is rising.

That is why movements can survive imperfect systems for a while, but they cannot survive a broken story for long. When a movement forgets what it is, or starts policing itself into silence, it loses the very thing that gave it influence in the first place. The audience doesn't punish you for being small. They punish you for being unclear.

What surprised me later is how often the same lesson shows up far from politics.

In Ethiopia, when the crusade collapsed into chaos, CfaN didn't scramble to protect an image. They moved — purposefully. The mission didn't die when the plan died because the plan had never been the point. They found the place where the purpose still lived and rebuilt the week around it. No panic. Just a steady relocation of the work to the ground that could still hold it.

And in Calcutta, I watched a different kind of positioning altogether. Ron Shaw's influence wasn't a strategy; it was a footprint. A school that educated thousands. A hospital that served a city. People stopped him in the street not because he had a title, but because his leadership had left something tangible behind.

Then Mother Teresa sat beside me on a wooden bench and reminded me — without trying — that moral authority is its own form of positioning. Her voice was barely audible. Yet everything in her presence carried weight, because she didn't need to persuade anyone she was aligned. She was.

That is the thread running through all of these stories: the deepest influence doesn't begin with visibility. It begins with coherence. It begins when your internal life and your external posture match closely enough that people trust what they're seeing.

Positioning, in the end, is not a trick of optics. It is what happens when

a leader chooses the right ground — and stays there — long enough for the story to take hold.

A closing discipline

Most leaders think influence comes from stepping farther into the light. Often it comes from stepping onto firmer ground.

Pay attention to where you instinctively reach for visibility, credit, or control — and ask what you're really trying to secure. Then choose the ground that aligns with purpose instead of ego, with mission instead of applause, with truth instead of momentum.

Because the outcomes that matter most are not always won at the podium. Many are shaped from the edges — by leaders who understood the frame, chose their ground wisely, and held their posture when the story tried to pull them somewhere easier.

CHOOSE YOUR GROUND

Influence doesn't always belong to the person in the spotlight. Sometimes it belongs to the one who understands the frame — who chooses the right ground, holds it under pressure, and quietly changes what everyone else has to account for.

Don't start with messaging. Start with meaning.

If you want the recall lesson to live inside your leadership, you don't begin by polishing the story. You begin by deciding what must remain true when the story gets noisy.

1. CHOOSE YOUR GROUND BEFORE YOU CHOOSE YOUR WORDS

Tom McClintock didn't try to out-entertain Arnold. He stood where his identity had weight: seriousness, clarity, conviction. That ground didn't make him the headline, it made him the stabilizing force.

Before your next high-stakes conversation or decision, ask:

- What am I standing for in this moment?
- What am I unwilling to trade for approval, speed, or applause?
- What "version of me" does this situation require — and what version would be easier but false?

Positioning begins when your posture is decided before your pitch.

2. SEPARATE PURPOSE FROM PLAN, AND PRACTICE THE PIVOT

In Ethiopia, the plan collapsed. The mission didn't. CfaN didn't cling to the broken structure; they moved to the place where the purpose could still breathe.

Do this in your own work:

- Name the mission in one sentence.

- Name the current plan in one sentence.
- Then ask: If the plan dies today, where does the mission still live — and what would faithfulness look like there?

Plans break. Purpose relocates.

3. REBUILD PRESENCE THROUGH RHYTHM, NOT INTENSITY

CRA regained weight because we became hard to ignore again, not with hype, but with steady, consistent presence. Messaging that arrived on time. A voice that reappeared month after month. A story that sounded like it knew who it was.

If your organization feels invisible, don't chase volume. Build rhythm:

- Show up predictably.
- Communicate consistently.
- Make your message substantive enough to carry weight.

Let repetition do what bursts of intensity can't. Influence grows when people can count on your presence.

4. ACCEPT THE COST OF EDGE INFLUENCE — AND REFUSE THE NEED FOR CREDIT

McClintock didn't win the office, but he changed the conditions. CRA didn't always get thanked, but it shaped how legislators and campaigns behaved. Some of the most decisive influence happens where the cameras aren't pointed.

Your test is simple:

- Can I shape the outcome without needing the headline?
- Can I do the quiet work and let someone else receive the visible win?
- Can I serve the mission more than my ego?

When you stop needing credit, you gain freedom — and your influence deepens.

A CLOSING DISCIPLINE

Pick one "edge position" you will hold this week. Not a role. A posture.

And here is what this requires of you when no one is watching: practice choosing the right ground before the room tests you. Decide in advance where you will not compromise for approval. Notice the places you crave credit. Confront the private hunger for visibility that turns good leadership into quiet negotiation with ego.

Then prove your posture in small ways: show up prepared, speak plainly, keep your micro-promises, hold the line on what matters without making a speech about it. Do the quiet work even if no one thanks you. Serve the mission without needing the headline.

One day you'll walk into a room where people aren't asking for a better message. They're asking whether anything is solid. If you've chosen your ground in advance — in private, in restraint, in integrity — you won't have to scramble for influence.

You'll already have it.

PART VI

RESTORATION, WONDER
& FUTURE STORY

CHAPTER 17

THE ROAD BACK TO WONDER

By the time 2015 arrived, Cathy and I had been discussing the idea of travel for more than two years. It began the way most impossible dreams begin — softly, almost jokingly, the kind of conversation you have late at night when the weight of the day feels a little too heavy and you wonder what life might look like if you closed one chapter and stepped quietly into another.

The world we had lived in for decades — campaigns, deadlines, relentless news cycles, the churn of California politics — had grown sharp around the edges. We weren't burned out exactly, but we were worn thin, more cynical than we wanted to admit, carrying a fatigue that didn't go away with sleep.

Our son had graduated from college and settled into a solid job. The house that once felt like a place of roots now felt like a reminder of a life we had already lived. And for the first time in years, we felt the freedom to ask the question: "What if we just went?"

And so we made the decision. We bought a forty-foot Winnebago Journey motorhome — fittingly named — and loaded it with only what mattered. We sold almost everything and rented out the house.

The plan was simple: travel for one year. We didn't know yet that one year would become seven.

ENTERING THE WIDE COUNTRY

Within the first few hundred miles, the noise of our old life began to fade. There is something strange and wonderful about watching your entire world shrink to what fits inside a motorhome. Every mile strips away what you thought you needed, leaving you with what you actually value.

What we found first wasn't scenery — it was people.

In campgrounds, highways, state parks, and grocery store parking lots, we met Americans who reminded us of the country beneath the noise. Mechanics and retirees, teachers and veterans, young couples living on tight budgets but rich in optimism. People who knocked on our door when our rig wouldn't level.

People who offered tools or advice without being asked. People who waved as we pulled out of a campsite, giving that unspoken blessing travelers exchange across miles and memory.

It struck me how quickly the cynicism we carried began to dissolve. The national storyline was one of fracture and hostility, but the lived reality was something different — something quieter, sturdier, more human.

And that revealed something about leadership: Leaders cannot lead what they no longer see.

We must step outside the echo chamber if we want to understand the people we claim to serve.

Wonder begins with seeing people again.

Wonder begins with seeing people again.

THE LAND THAT RESTORES PERSPECTIVE

The landscapes reshaped us next.

We had traveled through nearly every inch of California in our careers, but nothing prepared us for the sheer variability and immensity of the American canvas. One week we stood on the Hurricane Deck at Niagara Falls, soaked in mist, feeling the raw force of a continent's water collapsing into a single roar. Another week we hiked to Avalanche Lake in Glacier National Park, the mountains rising like stone cathedrals around us, their peaks scarred with the quiet persistence of time.

Utah stunned us the most. Zion, Bryce, Arches — each place a geological sermon on endurance and wonder.

The land had a way of recalibrating the soul. Campaign life shrinks your world to districts, messaging, deadlines, and demographics. But standing beneath a thousand-foot canyon wall or watching a thunderstorm race across the plains forces a different scale into view.

And that, too, is leadership: perspective is what keeps ambition from deforming into self-importance.

When you remember you are small, the work becomes big in the right way again.

THE MUSEUMS — HISTORY AS A MENTOR

Our love of history pulled us into museums in small towns and big cities alike. Some were quirky, like the Museum of Clean in Idaho, and some were heartbreaking, like the Mississippi Civil Rights Museum. But each one held something that shaped the way I saw leadership.

We didn't just rediscover America through people and landscapes. We rediscovered it through the stories the nation left behind.

GETTYSBURG

At Gettysburg, long glass walls displayed pre-war newspapers — columns of rhetoric so vicious, so divided, so unyielding, that I felt a chill. The nation had once spoken to itself in headlines dripping with contempt. We like to imagine our era is uniquely divided, but reading those pages revealed the uncomfortable truth: the fracture wasn't new. What was new was that our divisions had not yet demanded blood.

Standing there, I realized: Leadership is what determines whether a nation pulls itself back from the brink or tumbles into it.

Narratives can heal — or they can harden into battle lines.

THE WEIGHT PEOPLE DON'T TALK ABOUT

Throughout our travels, we met more than a few World War II veterans. None of them carried bravado. They didn't retell battles for applause or posture as heroes. They carried themselves with an understated firmness — a clarity in their eyes that said they had seen more than they would ever put into words. They were the embodiment of what we call the Greatest Generation, and most of them seemed almost allergic to honor.

It was personal for Cathy. Her dad had served aboard a submarine in the Pacific — the USS *Muskallunge* — but he never talked about it.

Walking through the Submarine Force Museum in Groton, Connecticut, we turned a corner and stopped cold. There, among the artifacts and black-and-white photos, was a commissioning picture of his boat — and his face in the middle of it. A few panels away, we learned what he had never told: depth-charge attacks, damage that forced the *Muskallunge* to limp into port in Australia for repairs, patrols that could easily have ended at the bottom of the ocean instead of in a quiet Midwestern life.

Standing there, I realized something about leadership I should have known sooner: The people you lead are carrying stories you may never hear.

Some have survived their own depth-charge days — medical diagnoses, combat tours, family implosions, private losses that never make it into an HR file or a leadership retreat icebreaker. Their calm isn't complacency; it's hard-won resilience. Their silence isn't emptiness; it's stewardship of pain that doesn't need an audience.

The people you lead are carrying stories you may never hear.

Leaders don't need all the details to lead people with honor. We simply need to assume there is more beneath the surface than we can see — and treat every person accordingly.

THE MISSISSIPPI CIVIL RIGHTS MUSEUM

In Jackson, Mississippi, we walked through the Civil Rights Museum and felt the weight of man's inhumanity laid bare — segregation, violence, injustice carved into the architecture of daily life. But woven through it were stories of courage that didn't roar but whispered — ordinary people taking extraordinary risks with no promise of safety.

It reminded me that the future doesn't bend toward justice by accident. Someone has to push.

THE SIXTH FLOOR MUSEUM

In Dallas, the Sixth Floor Museum at Dealey Plaza confronted us with a different kind of weight — a story whose ending was official but not settled. We left with more questions than answers, not because truth was hidden, but because history sometimes refuses neat explanations.

It taught me that leaders must live with ambiguity without losing integrity — a rare and necessary skill.

DON ASLETT & THE MUSEUM OF CLEAN

In Pocatello, Idaho, we ducked into the Museum of Clean expecting a diversion. What we found instead was a masterclass in alignment.

Don Aslett greeted us himself. The founder of the museum, he's a pioneer in the cleaning industry — a man who has written books, built companies, and spent decades teaching that cleanliness wasn't about sanitation alone; it's about dignity, stewardship, and responsibility. As he walked us through exhibits filled with antique vacuums, environmental displays, and stories of community transformation, something became clear: he didn't just *advocate* cleanliness; he *embodied* it.

His message had credibility because his life had continuity.

And that is leadership in its purest form: your message only carries as far as your alignment.

THE DESERT FLIGHT

Years after the Presidential motorcade — long after I thought I understood what intensity looked like — I found myself in a place that rewired my assumptions again. It was through the work of the ESGR, the Employer Support of the Guard and Reserve, a group dedicated to helping businesses understand why their people might be gone for weeks or months at a time in their service to the National Guard.

That's how I ended up in the Mojave Desert.

We began the day climbing into an old Huey, the kind of helicopter whose rotor wash carries a sound you feel in your chest. The pilot lifted us over the California foothills, and the familiar convenience of paved roads disappeared beneath us. ESGR trips weren't designed to impress. They were designed to break the distance between civilian assumptions and military reality.

We landed at a small base further south, dust still swirling when the doors slid open. Without much ceremony, we were moved from the Huey toward a waiting Chinook. The scale change was immediate — twin rotors, heavy-lift frame, the sense that the aircraft didn't simply take you somewhere but pulled you into its world.

Once we were airborne again, the Chinook dropped low over the Mojave. The rear ramp remained down the entire flight, nothing but desert wind and hot air rushing through the open bay. The noise inside was so loud it stripped away any impulse to narrate the moment. You just held on to the overhead strap and let the terrain rush beneath you — dry washes, scattered rocks, the pale trace of tracks disappearing into the horizon. The aircraft bucked and vibrated as if the desert itself were reminding us that real training doesn't happen on smooth ground.

We landed at the National Training Center and were led to a canvas tent where soldiers were taking a break between exercises. It was a room of folding chairs, tables, and MREs stacked in a bin. I sat with them, peeling open the brown packaging while they talked about their units and the training rotation they were in. The conversations were matter-of-fact, steady, completely free of the hedging I'd grown accustomed to in political rooms.

What stayed with me wasn't the laser-based weapons systems or the simulation technology — though both were impressive. It was the posture of these soldiers. Clarity was not something they searched for. It was something they carried. They knew why they were there. They knew what was expected. They weren't negotiating meaning every few minutes the way so many organizations do. Their mission didn't need branding or spin to make sense.

That contrast worked on me. On our return trip, the ramp stayed open again, the desert pouring past in late-afternoon color. It was the kind of moment that doesn't announce itself. It just settles into you. There, strapped in, I realized how much of my own disillusionment over the years had come from environments where clarity was optional, where purpose shifted depending on the room or the audience.

The soldiers I'd eaten lunch with didn't have that luxury. Their world didn't function if everyone interpreted the mission differently. In their environment, ambiguity wasn't interesting — it was dangerous.

I carried that home, not as a neat leadership lesson or a metaphor polished for a keynote. It came back with me the same way the desert dust settled on my clothes — quiet, unasked for, but unmistakable. It reminded me that leadership is restored by proximity, not by inspiration. When you stand close enough to people who live their purpose without theatrics, something in you recalibrates.

Years later, out on the road in our motorhome, I recognized that same recalibration happening again — not in helicopters or training ranges, but in campgrounds and quiet stretches of highway. Ordinary people, steady in who they were, doing what needed to be done.

The Mojave didn't give me a revelation. But looking back, it gave me clarity. And sometimes that's the thing you've been missing without realizing it.

THE BLOWOUT

Not every moment on the road was beautiful. One afternoon in Idaho, the front driver-side tire of our motorhome exploded at highway speed. The sound was less a pop than a detonation. The rig lurched violently.

When we finally came to a shaking stop, our electrical bay was torn apart, metal twisted and wires dangling like roots ripped from the earth. It took dozens of phone calls to find a tire and arrange delivery to the shoulder of the highway.

Then the service truck arrived.

The man who emerged was calm, focused, and utterly unfazed by danger. He knelt beside our motorhome — mere inches from eighty-mile-per-hour traffic — while the wash of passing trucks buffeted him with the force of a storm. He worked steadily, methodically, courage in motion but never announced.

Leadership sometimes looks like vision casting and speeches. But sometimes it looks like a man kneeling on hot asphalt, doing what must be done without applause.

Quiet courage saves more lives than loud heroism ever will.

Quiet courage saves more lives than loud heroism ever will.

LEADERSHIP PRINCIPLE — WHY WONDER IS A STRATEGIC ADVANTAGE

Leaders don't lose effectiveness all at once. They lose it slowly — through cynicism, fatigue, overexposure to conflict, or the quiet narrowing of perspective that happens when the world shrinks to deadlines, crises, and constant urgency.

The road restored something leadership had worn thin in me: wonder.

Wonder isn't sentimental. It's strategic. It clears the inner lens that responsibility clouds and widens perspective, where stress narrows it. It makes a leader see people again instead of problems. And it reawakens the curiosity that ambition often suffocates.

Leadership without wonder becomes mechanical.

Leadership with wonder becomes humane.

Here is the truth the miles taught me: Leaders cannot lead with clarity if they have forgotten how to see with wonder.

Wonder reopens the heart. Wonder recalibrates priorities. Wonder restores humility. Wonder returns a leader to presence — the most neglected leadership skill of our time.

By the time we sold the motorhome seven years later, I understood something I wish I had known decades earlier: A leader's life is not defined by the miles they travel, but by the meaning they gather along the way.

Meaning makes leadership sustainable.

Wonder makes leadership possible.

And together, they become the quiet force that shapes a legacy worth leaving.

CHAPTER 18

STORY AS LEGACY

There comes a point on any long journey — whether across a continent in a motorhome, across a career in politics, or across the shifting terrain of a life — when you begin to understand something you couldn't have learned earlier: legacy isn't the final chapter. It isn't the epilogue. It isn't the accomplishment list someone recites at your retirement dinner.

Legacy is the story you're living right now. The story that other people feel when they stand near you. The story that lingers long after your voice is gone.

Legacy is the story you're living right now.

I began to understand this somewhere between Glacier National Park and the rolling fields of Iowa, somewhere between the Sixth Floor Museum and the quiet hum of small-town libraries, somewhere between meeting strangers who became friends and revisiting memories that had shaped who I was long before I realized they were shaping me.

The truth crystallized slowly: people do not remember what you achieved — they remember how your life made meaning possible for them.

THE STORIES THAT OUTLAST US

One of the clearest moments came in Clear Lake, Iowa, inside the Surf Ballroom. The walls were lined with photographs of Buddy Holly, Ritchie Valens, and J.P. Richardson — three young men frozen in time by a plane crash on a cold February night. They were talented, bright, promising. But what struck me wasn't their fame. It was the way their music had lodged itself into the emotional vocabulary of the country. The songs they left behind helped people feel something about their own story.

That is what legacy is: the resonance you create in someone else's narrative. I felt that same resonance in Springfield, Illinois, standing inside the Abraham Lincoln Presidential Library. Lincoln didn't shape his life with an eye toward legacy. He carried wounds, doubts, and grief that would have crushed other men. But he kept orienting himself toward a larger moral story — and that alignment carved a direction for the nation that outlasted him by centuries. His legacy wasn't a monument. It was a narrative compass.

EVERYDAY LEGACIES

During our seven years on the road, Cathy and I met people whose legacies were small in scale but immense in meaning.

There was the trial attorney we'd become close friends with — the one who introduced himself as "just a small country lawyer," a line spoken with such disarming humility that you almost believed it. Around the picnic table, he was all warmth and easy stories, the kind of man who made strangers feel like old friends within minutes. His legacy wasn't the verdicts he'd won or the headlines he could have claimed, but the steady kindness that reassured us when we feared a fuel leak, and the way he treated every encounter, no matter how small, with generosity.

The Mennonite family, whose paths crossed ours in two different states, their modest grace and polite children reminding us how wonder thrives in simplicity.

The campground host who, when our water heater began leaking, was already halfway to his golf cart, saying, "Let me have a look." Within an hour, he'd found the right tool, patched the line, and turned what felt like a crisis into nothing more than another campfire story.

And the couple we spent two Easter mornings with — two different campgrounds, two different states — yet each holiday meal felt as if we were long-lost relatives welcomed back to the table.

None of these people were chasing platforms or titles. None of them imagined they were shaping anyone's future. Yet each held a story that quietly helped someone else understand who they were.

Legacy is rarely loud. Most of the time, it is lived in kitchens and garages and fishing docks, not boardrooms or podiums.

LEADERSHIP & LEGACY — WHY THE TWO ARE INSEPARABLE

The longer I live, the more convinced I am that leadership is simply legacy enacted in real time. People don't remember your talking points; they remember how you helped them interpret the world. They don't remember your strategies; they remember the clarity you brought into moments of confusion. They don't remember your authority; they remember your alignment.

I've seen this in politics, in ministry, in crisis, and in my own failures.

Ron Shaw didn't leave a legacy because he built a school or a hospital — though both still influence lives today. He left a legacy because his life *was* the message: integrity that shaped environments, humility that gave weight to his voice, a quiet steadiness that made people feel safe enough to grow.

Mother Teresa left a legacy because her whisper carried the weight of a life aligned with its purpose.

Rosa Parks left a legacy because her stillness — her refusal to rise from a seat that was rightfully hers — gave the country a clearer story about dignity than any speech could have.

Even my own painful chapter — the collapse of the film project, the financial unraveling that followed, the humbling that stripped away ego — became a kind of legacy. Not the kind you choose, but the kind that refines. The kind that teaches you to live a truer story than the one you were chasing. The kind that makes you more trustworthy because the shell of pretense finally cracked.

And I've seen the opposite too.

The congressional candidate whose biography felt off. Polished, rehearsed, incomplete. A story with deliberate blanks. And when the attack ads came, asking, "What do we really know about this man?" those blanks became black holes. He had left room for others to write his story for him — and they did.

Leaders lose the room when the story they live doesn't match the story they tell.

Leaders lose the room when the story they live doesn't match the story they tell.

LEGACY LIVES IN PEOPLE, NOT ACHIEVEMENTS

Legacy isn't in monuments or awards or titles or vote counts. It's in the daughter who discovers her father survived depth charges in the Pacific and walks a little taller knowing she comes from courage. It's in the couple who repairs an RV together on the side of an Idaho highway and realizes their marriage can withstand more than they imagined. It's in the strangers you meet on the road who start telling their stories differently because your life gave them room to interpret their own with more meaning.

Legacy lives in the people who carry a piece of your story forward without realizing they're doing it.

THE LEADERSHIP LESSON AT THE HEART OF IT ALL

And so, after decades of campaigns, crises, recoveries, adventures, and quiet moments on highways and mountaintops, here is the leadership truth I now believe more deeply than anything else in this book:

Your legacy is not measured by how many people remember your name. It's measured by how many people discovered their own story because you lived yours well.

Your clarity becomes someone else's courage.

Your integrity becomes someone else's compass.

Your presence becomes someone else's stability.

Your story becomes someone else's meaning.

That is the power of storytelling in leadership — not as performance, not as persuasion, but as inheritance. **The story you live becomes the story you leave.**

And long after your words fade, long after your accomplishments are forgotten, the meaning you helped others discover is what remains.

CHAPTER 19

THE ARCHITECTURE OF ACCOUNTABILITY

In the early 2000s, my world was full of ministries with big vision and even bigger language. Mailers talked about "world changers" and "nation shakers," phrases that could be prophetic or dangerous depending on the character of the people using them.

One of my clients in that season was a ministry led by a dynamic preacher I'll call "the evangelist." Onstage, he was magnetic — funny, intense, urgent. His heartbeat was sending high school and college students on short-term mission trips around the world. The imagery was compelling: young people fanning out across continents with unfiltered enthusiasm and a sense of purpose.

My role seemed simple. I designed their monthly newsletter, *World Changer*, and crafted materials that told the story — photos of students praying in villages, testimonies from schools overseas, maps with bright arrows arching across continents like flight paths of hope. From the outside, the ministry looked strong and full of momentum.

And then, almost without warning, it folded.

One day, the ministry unexpectedly closed its doors. No explanation. Just… silence. Its global mission ended with little ceremony. They even had a "fire sale" selling off all of the assets — computers, audio gear, cameras, the works.

For me, it barely registered in the moment. I had other clients calling and deadlines waiting. But for the students, volunteers, and staff who had traveled, prayed, and invested deeply, it was a gut punch. A sudden, bewildering end to something that had felt so alive.

At the time, it simply seemed odd.

It wouldn't be until several years later that the truth surfaced.

I remember the moment with absolute clarity — sitting at my desk, glancing up at the television, and catching a familiar face in the corner of my eye. That instant jolt of recognition, the brain connecting dots before the heart is ready. The name on the chyron was slightly different, but the man was unmistakably "the evangelist" whose stories I had once helped amplify, whose ministry materials I had designed with genuine belief in the work.

Now he was being indicted.

As the details unfolded — the name change, the hidden conviction, the investment schemes woven through religious language — that odd moment from years earlier suddenly clicked into place.

And the collapse wasn't organizational. It was moral. Spiritual. Human.

What stayed with me wasn't the legal complexity — that belonged to investigators and attorneys. What struck me was the cost borne by ordinary people. Students who believed they were part of a world-changing mission. Supporters who gave not from excess, but from sacrifice. Staff who built their lives, their identity, even their future, around a calling they trusted. Investors who were defrauded.

They weren't just grieving a failed ministry. They were grieving the betrayal of integrity.

For me, the news landed with a heaviness I didn't expect. I had once helped shape the outer shell of that story — the newsletters, the photos of smiling students, the hopeful headlines — all crafted in good faith, believing the narrative we had been handed. To watch it crumble was sobering. And it taught me a truth that has never left me:

A powerful story without corresponding character becomes a weapon.

A powerful story without corresponding character becomes a weapon.

It doesn't simply fail. It *fails people.*

The individuals who gave, served, traveled, and believed were not foolish. They were responding to the very values we celebrate — generosity, impact, bold faith. They were told their efforts were helping "change the world." But behind the inspiring language, something else had been quietly unraveling.

In the years that followed, I found myself listening differently.

When leaders used grand language but resisted simple accountability... When ministries celebrated impact but sidestepped transparency... When the public narrative grew louder even as the internal structure grew thinner...

I listened for humility. For alignment. For the quiet, unglamorous systems that tether a leader to truth when momentum tries to carry them beyond their character.

Because once you've watched a "world-changing" narrative implode under the weight of unconfessed compromise, you don't hear certain phrases the same way again.

Vision is not virtue.

Charisma is not character.

And eventually, the story you *live* will swallow the story you *sell*.

What I eventually learned is that collapses like this never come out of nowhere. They aren't sudden storms. They begin as slow drifts — small decisions made outside of counsel, outside of community, outside of prayer. They begin the moment a leader steps out from under the structures designed to protect both their soul and their story.

In every failure I've witnessed — and in the hardest seasons of my own journey — the pattern is the same: where accountability is absent, drift is inevitable.

Where accountability is absent, drift is inevitable.

But where accountability is present — deep, honest, structural, and spiritual — leaders don't simply avoid disaster. They stay aligned. Their influence stays clean. Their story remains whole.

And that is why the next principle matters so much.

It isn't dramatic or glamorous. But it is the difference between a leader who endures and a leader who fractures. It's the architecture of accountability.

Every leader carries two stories at once: the one they *tell* and the one they *live*. When those stories align, leadership becomes a force for good. When they drift apart, even by degrees, the distance between them eventually becomes a fault line. Over the years, I've come to believe that the difference between those two outcomes often comes down to one thing: accountability.

Accountability is not a restriction. It is a safeguard. It's the quiet framework — often unseen and rarely celebrated — that keeps a leader's integrity intact when pressure, opportunity, or fatigue begin to pull in the wrong direction. The healthiest leaders I've known didn't surround themselves with guardrails because they were weak. They did it because they understood how easy it is for any of us to wander without them.

There are three dimensions of accountability that shape a leader's inner life as much as their outer story.

1. STRUCTURAL ACCOUNTABILITY

Some leaders resist structure, viewing boards, bylaws, elders, and financial oversight as obstacles to speed or vision. But those systems exist for a reason. They slow decisions just enough to let wisdom speak. They create transparency where secrecy would prefer to live. And they prevent one person's momentum from becoming everyone else's mistake.

The organizations that weather crises, and the leaders who stay trustworthy, nearly always have these structures in place long before they need them.

2. RELATIONAL ACCOUNTABILITY

Every leader needs people around them who are willing to ask questions, raise concerns, and tell the truth even when it's uncomfortable. These relationships act as mirrors, revealing blind spots we'd rather not acknowledge and motives we might not see clearly on our own.

Some of the most resilient leaders I've known maintained friendships and peer relationships that outlasted their titles. Those voices helped them stay centered when success tempted them toward independence or when difficulty tempted them toward isolation.

But the opposite is also true. When a leader builds a circle that laughs at every joke, affirms every impulse, and never challenges the gap between public image and private behavior, the drift begins long before anyone notices.

I once saw this up close.

Years ago, I knew a motivational speaker who also served as a pastor. He was the kind of communicator who could lift the atmosphere of a room within minutes — funny, polished, confident. When he spoke, people walked away inspired. I invited him to speak at the Prayer Breakfast for the California Republican Assembly's annual convention, and the day before the event, he and his team were in the hotel lobby waiting for transportation.

He spotted one of the CRA members walking by — a kind, soft-spoken man wearing a cap embroidered with an eagle and an American flag. The

176

speaker called him over warmly, admired the hat, and asked where he found it, how long he'd had it, and what it meant to him. The conversation was friendly and genuine — or at least it appeared to be. When the gentleman walked away, he did so with a smile, clearly touched by the encounter.

As soon as he left, the speaker turned to his group and said, "What a chump. He really thought I liked his hat."

There was a ripple of awkward laughter — more compliance than agreement. No one challenged him. No one pulled him aside. And he didn't expect them to. The next morning, he delivered the same powerful, inspiring message he was known for. But for me, the veneer had cracked. I had seen the misalignment between the public story and the private posture.

It wasn't a scandal or a crisis. It was something smaller but revealing — a glimpse of what happens when a leader's circle no longer tells the truth. Without relational accountability, performance becomes substitution for character, and affirmation becomes a poor replacement for honesty.

3. SPIRITUAL ACCOUNTABILITY

For me, the seasons where my own leadership faltered were not marked by dramatic crises but by a slow shift in posture. I moved from seeking God's direction to assuming I already knew it. Decisions that once came out of prayer came instead from instinct or urgency. It wasn't rebellion; it was drift — quiet, subtle, and easy to miss until the consequences arrived.

Spiritual accountability is the discipline of remaining teachable before God. It's the practice of giving Him access not just to your conclusions but to your motives. When that posture slips, everything else eventually follows.

WHY ACCOUNTABILITY MATTERS

Accountability, in all its forms, acts as a tether. It keeps a leader grounded when success accelerates or when challenges mount. It prevents the inner story from being overtaken by the outer one. It offers perspective at the very moments when perspective is hardest to find.

Most importantly, accountability preserves trust. Trust is the true currency of leadership, and once it's lost, no amount of talent, charisma, or public narrative can replace it.

Over the years, I've learned that leaders rarely fail because of a single catastrophic decision. They fail because of a long sequence of unchallenged ones. Accountability interrupts that sequence. It creates the space for reflection, course correction, confession, and humility — long before collapse becomes inevitable.

In the end, accountability is not about restraint; it's about alignment. It ensures the story we are telling with our words matches the story we are living with our lives. And when those two stay close — when character supports calling and humility keeps ambition steady — leadership becomes not only more effective, but more deeply human. It becomes the kind of leadership people can trust, follow, and remember long after the spotlight fades.

WONDER RECOVERED

By the time Cathy and I pulled away from our driveway in that motorhome, I was carrying an exhaustion I didn't know how to name. It wasn't the fatigue of overwork. It was the fatigue of disillusionment — the kind that accumulates when you've lived too long inside conflict, too close to deadlines, too near the sharp edges of public life.

It was a cynicism that had settled in almost unnoticed, the kind many political professionals learn to wear as armor. Campaigns train you to see everything as leverage. Crisis trains you to narrow your focus. Over time, without meaning to, you stop expecting beauty.

The road didn't fix that overnight, but it began to unwind it.

Something happens when your life shrinks to what fits inside a motorhome. You stop pretending you need what you don't. You stop polishing what doesn't matter. You start noticing what you've been walking past. In campgrounds and grocery store parking lots and state parks, we met Americans who didn't resemble the national storyline. People offered tools without being asked. They knocked on the door when the rig wouldn't level. They waved as we pulled out, the unspoken blessing travelers exchange when they'll never meet again but still want the other person to make it.

It struck me how quickly cynicism dissolves when you're forced back into proximity with real people. The loudest narrative said the country was only anger and fracture. The lived reality was quieter and sturdier than that. And it reminded me of something leadership can forget: **you cannot lead what you no longer see.** If your world becomes an echo chamber, your leadership becomes a performance for people you've reduced to categories.

Then the land began restoring perspective.

Campaign life shrinks the world to districts and messaging and urgency. But standing beneath a canyon wall that makes your calendar feel ridiculous forces a different scale into view. The immensity doesn't diminish the importance of your work; it corrects the way you carry it. Perspective is what keeps responsibility from turning into self-importance. When you remember you are small, the work becomes big in the right way again.

And then there were the museums — history as a mentor, not a hobby.

Gettysburg wasn't simply a battlefield; it was a mirror. Those pre-war newspapers were so vicious, so hardened, that I felt the chill of what words can become when they are no longer restrained by responsibility. The Mississippi Civil Rights Museum reminded us that the future doesn't bend toward justice by accident. Someone has to push, often at great cost, and rarely with applause. The Sixth Floor Museum left us with ambiguity we couldn't resolve, and that, too, was a lesson: leaders have to live with unanswered questions without losing integrity.

But the deepest moments weren't the most scenic.

They were the veterans who carried their history without bravado, not empty, but disciplined, as if they were stewarding pain that didn't need an audience. They were the moment in Groton when we found Cathy's father, frozen in a commissioning photograph, and discovered details he'd never told: depth charges, damage, patrols that could have ended at the bottom of the Pacific. Standing there, I realized how many people are living with "depth-charge days" no one will ever put into words — diagnoses, losses, betrayals, private wars that never make it into an HR file or a leadership retreat icebreaker. Leaders don't need all the details to lead with honor. We simply need to assume there is always more beneath the surface than we can see, and treat people accordingly.

And then there was the tire blowout in Idaho — violent, sudden, humbling. A reminder that the road isn't a montage. It's real life. When the technician arrived, he knelt inches from highway traffic, calm and focused, as if danger was simply part of the job. His courage wasn't loud. It didn't ask to be noticed. It just did what needed to be done.

Somewhere in those miles, the principle of Part VI began to crystallize: **wonder is not sentimental. It's strategic.** It clears the inner lens that responsibility clouds. It widens perspective where stress narrows it. It restores humility before ambition has a chance to deform into something brittle.

But wonder alone isn't enough.

I've also seen what happens when a story is powerful but the structure beneath it is thin. I watched a ministry collapse not from external opposition but from internal compromise. I watched a communicator speak with conviction onstage and mock a man the moment he walked away, and I realized how quickly public virtue can become private contempt when no one is close enough to tell the truth. I've watched drift happen in my own life, not through rebellion, but through subtle independence — the quiet move from seeking God to assuming I already knew what He would say.

That's why restoration in leadership has to become more than a season of refreshment. It has to become a way of living.

Wonder keeps you human. Accountability keeps you true. And when those two live together, a future story begins to form — not as branding, not as a five-year plan, but as an internal trajectory: a life becoming coherent again.

The leaders who endure aren't the ones who never tire. They're the ones who know how to recover sight before cynicism becomes identity, and how to rebuild structure before drift becomes collapse. Their leadership stops being primarily about what they accomplish and starts becoming about what their presence makes possible in the people around them.

That is restoration. That is wonder. That is the responsibility of the future story.

RESTORATION THAT ENDURES

Every leader eventually faces a season that depletes them — not through a single crisis, but through the slow accumulation of conflict, disappointment, and responsibility carried too long without renewal. You keep functioning, but something inside you dims. Your team feels it. Your decisions grow heavier. Your world shrinks.

Earlier sections focused on what leaders do. This one focuses on how leaders endure.

Restoration is not escape. It's recalibration. It's the return to the ground that makes sustainable leadership possible.

1. REOPEN YOUR VISION: STEP BACK INTO PROXIMITY WITH REAL PEOPLE

Cynicism grows in closed systems. When your world becomes an echo chamber, people slowly turn into categories — problems to solve, obstacles to manage, audiences to persuade.

Restoration begins when you deliberately re-enter human proximity.

Spend time with people who don't share your professional language. Listen to stories you wouldn't normally hear. Walk into places where you aren't in charge, where you can't control the frame, where you're forced to notice what you've been missing. Assume there is more beneath the surface of every person than you can see, because there is.

This is not a sentimental exercise. It is leadership maintenance. When you see people again, your leadership becomes human again.

2. RECOVER SCALE: REBUILD PERSPECTIVE BEFORE URGENCY BECOMES YOUR RELIGION

Leaders lose effectiveness when the current crisis becomes the whole world. Perspective doesn't minimize your challenges; it reframes them, so they don't consume you.

Create practices that restore scale. Study history, especially moments when division and pressure were worse than what you are currently facing. Spend time in places that remind you the world is larger than your calendar — nature, museums, biographies, long stretches without noise. Let your mind remember that your moment is real, but not ultimate.

When you recover perspective, urgency stops controlling you. You become steady enough to carry responsibility without being crushed by it.

3. BUILD GUARDRAILS: MAKE ACCOUNTABILITY STRUCTURAL, RELATIONAL, AND SPIRITUAL

If you've ever watched a compelling story collapse, you learn this quickly: failure rarely comes from one catastrophic decision. It comes from a long sequence of unchallenged ones.

Restoration that lasts requires accountability that holds when you're tired, celebrated, pressured, or alone.

Build structural accountability: oversight with real authority, financial transparency that doesn't depend on your good intentions, and decision-making that requires multiple voices.

Build relational accountability: friendships that outlast your title, people who can tell you the truth when your private posture starts drifting from your public message.

Build spiritual accountability: a teachable posture before God, where prayer is honest, not polished, and Scripture is allowed to confront, not just comfort.

Accountability isn't restriction. It's protection. It keeps the story you live from drifting away from the story you tell.

4. PROTECT WONDER: TREAT IT AS A DISCIPLINE, NOT A MOOD

Wonder is not a personality trait. It's a practice.

Reintroduce beauty into your leadership life on purpose. Engage with art, history, music, and the natural world without trying to turn them into productivity. Let yourself be moved by stories that aren't yours. Make room for moments that don't advance your goals but restore your soul.

Wonder clears the lens. It widens the frame. It reawakens curiosity, which is one of the first casualties of fatigue. And it restores humility, which keeps your leadership from becoming brittle.

Leaders who lose wonder don't become evil. They become mechanical. And mechanical leadership may be efficient, but it is rarely trustworthy.

A CLOSING DISCIPLINE

Measure your restoration by coherence, not by emotion. You don't need to feel inspired every day. You need your inner story and outer story to stay close enough that people can trust what they experience when they stand near you.

Here is what this requires of you when no one is watching: return to the practices that widen your vision and keep your soul accountable. Put yourself back in proximity to real people. Rebuild scale. Re-enter wonder on purpose. Keep the guardrails strong, not as image management, but as protection against drift. Pray honestly when there is no audience. Stay teachable when there is no crisis, forcing humility.

Return often to places where performance is unnecessary, and honesty is unavoidable. Keep your vision wide. Keep wonder alive. Keep your posture humble before God.

Because when pressure returns, and it always does, **your leadership will not rise to the level of your intentions. It will fall back to the level of your alignment.**

Restoration is how you make sure it falls back onto something solid, built quietly, daily, when no one is watching.

EPILOGUE

RETURN TO
THE MOTORCADE

When I stepped into the presidential motorcade, I mistook the spectacle for the lesson.

I was young and still wide-eyed enough to think leadership lived in the parts people noticed first. The engines humming in unison. The choreography of vehicles sliding into position. The clipped, disciplined voices on the radio. The agents scanning rooftops with a kind of stillness that felt almost cinematic. Even the smell of jet fuel on the Detroit tarmac seemed charged with significance.

It felt like power — the purest form of it.

Power arranged into motion.

Power wrapped in precision.

Power announcing itself in flashing lights and shut-down freeways.

But years later, after everything — the victories that lifted us, the losses that broke us, the film that collapsed, the business that nearly did, the motorhome miles that restored our wonder, the leaders whose quiet courage reshaped my own — I found myself looking back at that same formation with very different eyes.

The spectacle was never the point. It was only the surface.

What held the motorcade together wasn't authority. It wasn't command, or even the choreography.

It was story.

Every vehicle in a motorcade has a role, but roles only work when each driver understands the narrative they're part of — why they're there, what their movement protects, and how their choices either strengthen or destabilize the mission. The motorcycles at the front don't surge ahead because they feel important. The follow-up car doesn't drift because it's impatient. The lead vehicle doesn't move forward until the moment the story calls for it.

Motion without meaning is chaos.

Meaning turns motion into mission.

I didn't grasp that at twenty. I only knew my job: keep formation, keep a steady pace, don't tap the brakes with a network cameraman hanging out the open tailgate behind me. At the time, I thought that was enough — mechanics without meaning. The learning came years later after I watched campaigns fracture because no one shared the same story... after a movement splintered because its leaders had forgotten theirs... after my own life collapsed under the weight of a story I was trying too hard to control.

It came after seeing Rosa Parks' actual bus in the Henry Ford Museum and realizing her power had nothing to do with volume or force. It was alignment — a woman sitting in the seat that was rightfully hers, refusing to surrender her place in the story she already belonged to.

It came after listening to Mother Teresa, her presence bending the moral gravity of the moment by simply being congruent with the life she had chosen. "The work never ends."

It came after Ethiopia, when chaos became clarity because Reinhard Bonnke understood something few leaders do — when the story is clear, crisis is just another chapter.

It came after the Michigan gubernatorial campaign, when Michael Brown chose integrity over ambition because he refused to be written into someone else's scandal.

It came on the side of an Idaho highway, when a quiet technician knelt beside my blown tire as traffic whipped by at eighty miles an hour — a reminder that heroism is often the story no one sees.

And it came through Cathy, whose suffering taught me more about strength than any political victory ever had. Her story, lived faithfully in the shadows, shaped mine in ways no spotlight ever could.

Slowly, I realized what the motorcade had been trying to teach me all along:

You don't hold a formation together by force. You hold it together by story.

You don't hold a formation together by force
You hold it together by story.

Story is what tells people where they belong.
Story is what reveals what's at stake.

Story is what aligns individuals into a collective purpose — a family, a team, an organization, a nation, a movement.

The best leaders aren't the loudest voices in the convoy. They are the ones who understand and embody the story everyone else is following.

When story is clear, people move with confidence.

When story is confused, people hesitate, scatter, or turn on each other.

When story is absent, something else fills the void — fear, ego, noise, chaos.

Looking back now, I no longer see the limousine on I-94. I see the invisible narrative that made the whole moment possible.

I see the same pattern in every chapter of this book.

Reagan didn't persuade with policy alone. He gave the country a story of possibility.

Kemp didn't inspire by force of intellect. He offered a story of economic dignity.

Bonnke didn't reach continents because of charisma. He embodied a story of uncompromising faith and purpose.

Rosa Parks didn't change history through defiance. She changed it through the clarity of knowing exactly whose story she was living.

And I, who once thought leadership was the spectacle, learned that it was the story beneath it all along.

You, the reader, carry a story too.

A story that can hold a formation together.

A story that can steady a room.

A story that can restore what cynicism tries to erode.

A story that becomes legacy long before anyone names it so.

Leadership is not the vehicle at the front of the convoy. Leadership is the narrative that gives each vehicle its place and each person their purpose.

So I return to the motorcade one last time — not as the young man dazzled by the spectacle, but as someone who finally understands its language.

The engines still hum. The radios still crackle. The formation still moves with precision. But now I see what I couldn't see then: none of it holds together without the story.

Leadership is not the vehicle at the front of the convoy. Leadership is the narrative that gives each vehicle its place and each person their purpose.

And your story — lived clearly, lived courageously, lived with integrity — is the greatest leadership tool you will ever possess.

Thank you for walking this journey with me.

ACKNOWLEDGMENTS

This book reflects years of lessons learned, conversations shared, and stories lived. I'm grateful to the many leaders, colleagues, and friends who shaped my understanding of narrative, clarity, and influence along the way.

To Dr. Ron Shaw, whose quiet humility and unwavering steadiness shaped both my storytelling and my character. He opened an entire world of ministry to me. Because of his trust and calm, humble presence, I found myself standing in villages and cities I never imagined I'd see — India, Ethiopia, Indonesia, Hong Kong, Thailand, and many others. Those journeys reshaped my understanding of service, compassion, and the power of story. His influence is woven into this book in ways he would never point to, and that is precisely why it matters so much.

To Brenda Palmateer, my middle school drama teacher and an early mentor who saw ability in me long before I recognized it in myself. She trusted me with leading roles, challenged me to step forward, and helped build my confidence in front of an audience.

To Professor Ray Tanter at the University of Michigan, who opened my eyes to the world of international security affairs. Through his guidance, I traveled to Washington for briefings at the State Department and Pentagon and experienced moments, including a Marine One landing, that transformed abstract ideas into lived reality. His teaching sharpened my understanding of how decisions ripple far beyond the room where they are made.

To Professor George Grassmuck, whose class on the American presidency remains one of my favorites. He encouraged rigorous debate and welcomed disagreement. He valued the exchange of ideas, modeling the kind of intellectual humility and confidence that true leadership requires.

To Mike Spence, who passed far too young — a close friend and business partner whose insight and strategic thinking shaped some of the most meaningful chapters of my professional life. I still find myself reaching for his voice in moments when clarity is needed. His absence is felt, but his influence endures.

To Craig Forrest, whose friendship, calm-under-pressure presence, and generous creativity shaped how I approach both work and the world.

To Clark Durant and Andy Anuzis, who gave a wide-eyed college student his first opportunity to step into the world of politics — an open door that changed the course of my life.

To John Feliz, whose long-standing friendship and trust came at exactly the right moment. When I returned to politics, it was John who brought the first several campaigns my way — opportunities that relaunched me and reshaped the trajectory of my work.

To Wayne Johnson, partner, collaborator, and co-conspirator in countless campaigns — victories worth celebrating and losses worth learning from.

My deepest gratitude goes to my family.

To my dad, who gave me a love of travel and a curiosity about the world that shaped both my work and my worldview.

To my mom, who introduced me to television and opened the door to storytelling long before I understood what it would mean for my life.

To my son Zack, whose creativity knows no bounds and whose resilience in the face of challenges continually inspires me. In moments that would break others, he stands steady. Watching the way he builds, imagines, and presses forward has taught me as much about leadership as any classroom or campaign.

To my daughter Shannon, whose wide-eyed optimism carried her across the world — from Hong Kong to Mozambique — as a young missionary. Our long theological conversations have challenged me and sharpened me. She has built a successful career, but it's her generous spirit that stands out most.

And to my wife, Cathy, whose strength and steady presence made this work possible. She has walked through seasons of profound physical challenge with a courage that continues to humble me. And yet, anyone who knows her also knows the other side of that strength: the laughter, the openness, the genuine warmth that fills every room she enters. Cathy has never met a stranger; she gathers people with ease, disarms them with joy, and reminds me daily what it means to live wholeheartedly. Her life — boldly, faithfully lived, with a beauty that needs no spotlight — has shaped mine more than any platform ever could.

Above all, I give thanks to God — through Jesus Christ — for the restoration, correction, and clarity that emerged from seasons I did not expect. My faith is not an accessory to this work; it is the foundation beneath it. In moments of failure, confusion, and rebuilding, Christ remained faithful when I was not, steady when I was uncertain, and patient when I needed far more time than I deserved. Whatever clarity or usefulness these pages may offer is rooted first in grace received, not wisdom earned.

Any errors that remain are mine alone.

ABOUT THE AUTHOR

Jeff Evans is a storyteller, strategist, and producer whose career has spanned politics, ministry, and media for more than thirty years. His passion for narrative began early when, at thirteen, he floor-directed a live television broadcast — igniting a lifelong love for visual communication.

Jeff's story has taken him from the White House lawn as the President departed for Camp David to the leper colonies of Ethiopia, the markets of Hong Kong, and the volcanic ridges of Maui. He has met world leaders, stood alongside cultural icons such as Rosa Parks and Mother Teresa, and observed the world's complexities up close — from military briefings at the Pentagon to sunrise ceremonies on the banks of the Ganges.

His creative work has earned more than two dozen awards, including twenty-three Pollie Awards, four Telly Awards, and an ADDY. As a screenwriter, Jeff has been honored internationally: The Midnight Train won the Gold Prize for Best Historical Screenplay at the PAGE Awards, Traveling Light placed in the Kairos Prize for Spiritually Uplifting Screenplays, and The King Affair was named a finalist in the same competition.

Jeff and his wife, Cathy, spent seven years traveling the country in their motorhome, an experience they chronicled on their blog, *Adventures Along the Way*. They now reside in Florida, where Jeff continues helping leaders communicate with clarity, purpose, and story-driven leadership.

CONNECT WITH JEFF EVANS

For speaking inquiries, visit:
whoisjeffevans.com/speaking

For leadership content, resources, and updates:
whoisjeffevans.com

Twin Tails Press is an imprint of JC Evans, Inc.
For more information, visit
twintailspress.com

www.ingramcontent.com/pod-product-compliance
Lightning Source LLC
Chambersburg PA
CBHW050239270326
41914CB00041BA/2045/J

www.ingramcontent.com/pod-product-compliance
Lightning Source LLC
Chambersburg PA
CBHW050239270326
41914CB00041BA/2045/J